THE WORLD ALMANAC®

CHILDREN'S Treasury of Records and Facts

THE WORLD ALMANAC®

CHILDREN'S Treasury of Records and Facts

Margo McLoone-Basta, Alice Siegel and
Edward Fox

Ravette London

First published in the United States of America by
World Almanac Publications
Newspaper Enterprise Association
A division of United Media Enterprises
A Scripps Howard company
200 Park Avenue
New York, New York 10166

This edition published by Ravette Limited 1986
by arrangement with Pharos Books
Phototypeset by Input Typesetting Limited
Printed and bound in Great Britain for Ravette Limited
3 Glenside Estate, Star Road, Partridge Green,
Horsham, Sussex RH13 8RA
by Cox & Wyman, Reading

ISBN 0 948456 33 7

Contents

ACKNOWLEDGEMENTS

The Editor of this edition had the invaluable assistance of numerous people and organisations which willingly supplied information and answered queries. Special thanks are due to Anne Fleissig, Dr. Ann Foxell, Patricia Hingston, Patrick Moore, Sally Rhodes, and Ann White, and to the following organisations: Bank of England, British Library, International Union for Conservation and Natural Resources, Lloyds of London, London Symphony Orchestra, Longleat Safari Park, Metal Exchange, Music Weekly, National Book League, National Committee of the Youth Library Group of the Library Association, National Westminster Bank, Nature Conservancy Council, Population Concern, Royal Exchange, Royal Mint, Royal National Institute for the Blind, R.S.P.C.A., Seaby Ltd., Society of West End Theatre Managers, Stock Exchange, Warrior Association, Woburn Wild Life Kingdom, Whipsnade Park, World Wildlife Fund, and Zoological Society of London.

THE WORLD ALMANAC ®

CHILDREN'S Treasury of Records and Facts

Animals the World Over

An animal must be able to move, obtain food and oxygen, get rid of unwanted waste, make a place for itself in its environment, and reproduce to make a next generation.

Almost every part of the earth is inhabited by animal life. There are over a billion different varieties (species) of animals. To make it easier to study animals, scientists have divided them into groups. The two main groups are: animals with backbones and animals without backbones. A backbone is made up of small bones called vertebrae. Animals

with backbones are called vertebrates. Animals without backbones are called invertebrates. The vertebrates make up about 90 percent of all the animals in the world and are more complicated animals because they have nervous system.

The following is a partial list of vertebrates and invertebrates.

VERTEBRATES

Species	*Main Characteristics*
FISH Eel, flounder, perch, seahorses, sharks, tuna	Covered with scales, bony plates, or skin; live in water; breathe with gills; swim with fins (except for eels which use body muscles); cold-blooded.
AMPHIBIANS Frogs, newts, salamanders, toads	Covered with moist skin, not scales; live in water and breathe with gills as a baby; adults have lungs and live on land; cold-blooded.
REPTILES  Crocodiles, lizards, snakes, turtles	Covered with dry scales or bony plates; lay eggs; cold-blooded (body temperature changes according to weather),
BIRDS Chickens, peacocks, penguins, sparrows, swans, turkeys	Feathers; ability to fly, except for the following 6 non-flying birds: cassowary, ostrich emu, penguin kiwi, rhea
MAMMALS Bats, cattle, cats, dogs, horses, monkeys, whales	Body hair; warm-blooded (constant body temperature whether in a warm or cold place); young fed milk from mother's mammary glands.

INVERTEBRATES

Species	*Main Characteristics*
PROTOZOA (The simplest form of all animal life)	Single celled; invisible to the naked eye; live chiefly in water or on other animal bodies as a parasite.
SPONGES* Spongia mollissima (common bath sponge), sycon	They are usually sedentary and move very little; live in water.
COELENTERATES Corals, jelly fish, sea anemones	Bodies have large central cavity called coelenteron; live in water.
ECHINODERMS Starfish, sea corals	Bodies are star shaped with five points and have spiny skin; live in water.
WORMS **Flatworms**: flukes, tapeworms	All have long narrow bodies. Body is flat; move by creeping; live in water, on land, and on other animal bodies.
Roundworms: hookworms, trichinia	Body is spindle-like and whitish in colour; move by whiplike contortions; live in water, on land and on other animal bodies.
Jointed worms: angleworms, earthworms, leeches	Body is made up of a row of rings; move by creeping; live in water and in soil.
Rotifers: conchilus, philodina	Body has two circles of hairlike bristles. In motion they look like wheels. Microscopic but may be seen with the naked eye; live in water and on animal bodies.
MOLLUSCS Clams, oysters, slugs, snails	Body is soft, usually enclosed in a hard limy shell; live in water and on land.

****An animal that looks like a plant***

Species	*Main Characteristics*
ARTHROPODS **Crustaceans**: barnacles, crabs, crayfish, lobster, shrimp	Segmented body; body skeleton is on the outside. Have pairs of jointed legs; most live in water and breathe with gills.
Myriapods: centipedes, millipedes	Have 15 pairs or more of jointed legs; live on land.
Arachnids: mites, scorpions, spiders, ticks	Have 4 pairs of jointed legs, 2 body parts; most live on land.
INSECTS* Ants, bees, beetles, bugs, butterflies, silkworms	Have 3 pairs of jointed legs, 3 body parts; live in most places on earth.

***More species than all other animals (and plants) combined**

Animals Which Is Which?

ALLIGATORS AND CROCODILES
The major difference between alligators and crocodiles is the snout. The crocodile has a long, tapered snout, which narrows sharply from the eyes to the end of its nose. The alligator's snout is rounded. It is almost as broad at the end of the nose as at the eyes.

CAMELS, ONE AND TWO-HUMPED
The one-humped camel is known as a dromedary. The dromedary, because of its long legs, is taller. It is native to India and North Africa. The two-humped camel is a Bactrian and lives in China, Turkey, and Mongolia.

ELEPHANTS, AFRICAN AND ASIAN
The most obvious difference between Asian and African elephants is size. African elephants are much larger than Asian elephants. Also, African elephants have enormous floppy ears. The Asian elephant has a strongly arched back and four toenails on each of its hind feet. The African elephant's back is not arched and it has three toenails on each of its hind feet.

FROGS AND TOADS
Frogs have moist, smooth skin, and are great jumpers. Toads have dry, rough skin. They move around by clumsy, short hops.

INSECTS AND BUGS
A bug is one kind of insect. It has features that set it apart from other insects. A bug's front pair of wings is larger than the back pair and the sucking mouth parts arise from the front of the head. Other insects that are similar to bugs have large front wings and sucking mouth parts that arise from the back of the head.

MONKEYS—OLD WORLD AND NEW WORLD
The two types of monkeys are Old World (Asia and Africa) and New World (South America and Central America). The difference between these two types is the tail. The New World monkeys have grasping (holding) tails; Old World monkeys do not.

PUMAS, CATAMOUNTS, COUGARS AND MOUNTAIN LIONS
These are all names for the same animal; a large brown cat.

RHINOCEROS—AFRICAN AND INDIAN
The Indian Rhinoceros has one horn; the African Rhinoceros has two horns.

SKUNKS AND POLECATS
The American shunk has a white stripe down its back. The European polecat, its cousin, does not have a stripe.

TURTLES, TORTOISES, AND TERRAPINS
All of these reptiles can be called turtles in a general sense. Turtles that live on land all the time are called tortoises. Fresh water turtles that are edible are called terrapins. All other fresh and salt water species are called turtles.

Animal Names

Animal	*Group*	*Male*	*Female*	*Baby*
Ass	Pace	Jack	Jenny	Foal
Bear	Sloth	Boar	Sow	Cub
Cat	Cluster	Tom	Queen	Kitten
Cattle	Herd/Drove	Bull	Cow	Calf
Chicken	Clutch/Brood	Cock	Hen	Chick
Deer	Herd	Buck	Doe	Fawn
Donkey	Herd/Drove	Jackass/ Jack	Jenny	Foal
Dog	Kennel/Pack	Dog	Bitch	Pup
Duck	Flight/Flock	Drake	Duck	Duckling
Elephant	Herd	Bull	Cow	Calf
Fox	Skulk/Lead	Dog	Vixen	Cub
Goose	Gaggle	Gander	Goose	Gosling
Giraffe	Herd	Bull	Cow	Calf
Hare	Down/Husk/ Trip	Jack	Jill	Leveret
Horse	Team/Herd	Stallion	Mare	Foal
Kangaroo	Troop/ Herd/Mob	Buck	Doe	Joey
Lion	Pride	Lion	Lioness	Cub
Pig	Litter	Boar	Sow	Piglet
Quail	Bevy	(Adult)	(Adult)	Chick
Rabbit	Nest	Buck	Doe	Bunny
Seal	Herd/Bob	Bull	Cow	Pup
Sheep	Flock	Ram	Ewe	Lamb
Swan	Flock	Cob	Pen	Cygnet
Tiger	Ambush	Tiger	Tigress	Cub

Turkey	Flock	Tom	Hen	Poult
Whale	Pod	Bull	Cow	Calf
Wolf	Pack	Dog	Bitch	Cub
Zebra	Herd	Stallion	Mare	Colt

SCIENTIFIC NAMES

Scientists have given animals official names. These names differ from the animal's common name. Below is a list of descriptive English words based on the animal's scientific name.

apian	like a bee	**leonine**	like a lion
avian	like a bird	**lupine**	like a wolf
bovine	like a cow	**ovine**	like a sheep
canine	like a dog	**simian**	like an ape
equinine	like a horse	**taurine**	like a bull
feline	like a cat	**ursine**	like a bear

Animal Champions

Fastest

Bird	**Indian Swift**	200 miles per hour
Land animal	**Cheetah**	70 miles per hour
Ocean swimmer	**Sailfish**	68 miles per hour

Slowest

Fish (marine)	**Sea Horse**	10½ inches per minute
Animal	**Snail**	2 to 3 ft. per minute
Mammal	**Three-toed Sloth**	6 to 8 ft. per minute
Reptile	**Tortoise**	15 ft. per minute

Largest

Animal (living or extinct)	**Blue Whale** 100 ft. long	150 tons
Fish	**Whale Shark** 45 ft. long	13 tons
Land animal	**African Bull Elephant** 10 ft. tall	6 tons
Reptile	**Saltwater Crocodile** 16 ft. long	1,150 pounds
Freshwater fish	**Pirarucu** 15 ft. long	500 pounds
African cat	**Lion** 10 ft. long	500 pounds
Bird	**Ostrich** 8 ft. tall	300 pounds
Lizard	**Komodo Dragon** 10 ft. long	200 pounds
Rodent	**Water hog (Capybara)** 4 ft. long	150 pounds

Amphibian	**Giant Salamander** 5 ft. long	100 pou
Flying Bird	**Condor** 15 ft. (wingspan)	25 pounds
Frog	**Goliath** 1 ft. long	10 pounds

Animal Words and Phrases in the English Language

Animals have personalities and special traits. People use the animal world to enrich their language. Just the mention of an animal can provide a colourful description of people or events. Here is a partial listing of animal words and phrases along with their meanings.

	Meaning	*Origin*
Bee	A social gathering for work like a sewing bee	Bees are busy animals that word hard together.
Black Sheep	An outcast	The wool of a black sheep has little value because it is difficult to dye.
Clam up	To be silent	The mouth of the clam is difficult to open.
Crocodile tears	Fake crying	Legend has it that crocodiles attracted their victims by crying.
Dead as a dodo	Not alive	Dodo birds are now extinct.

	Meaning	*Origin*
Dog	To trail persistently	Dogs are used to hunt other animals.
Duck	To plunge under water, or to dodge	Ducks in water frequently bob their heads beneath the water.
Eager Beaver	One who is overly enthusiastic	Beavers are known for being extremely hard workers.
Ferret	To hunt out	Ferrets are animals well-known for hunting rodents.
Fox	A sly person	Foxes are known for their trickiness.
Get your goat	To become irritated	Goats were often stabled with thoroughbred racing horses to calm them. Horses who were used to having the goats around would become very upset when the goats were removed.
Goose pimples	Bumps on the skin when one is frightened or cold	The flesh of a goose is pimpled after its feathers have been plucked.
Guinea pig	Someone who is sacrificed to further a plan	Guinea pigs are commonly used in scientific experiments.
Hightail it	Make a fast getaway	Rabbits and many other animals raise their tails high when running from danger.
Hold your horses	Be patient	Horse drivers in county fair races often started their horses before the race had begun. Spectators would shout 'Hold your horses!'
Horsepower	A unit of power in mechanics	The power a horse uses in pulling.

	Meaning	*Origin*
Pigeonhole	To file away for future use	Old-fashioned desks had compartments called pigeon-holes because they looked like nesting holes in dovecots.
Play possum	To pretend or deceive	Possums (opossums) pretend they are dead when threatened or captured.
Smell a rat	To suspect something	Cats have the ability to smell rats they cannot see.
Squirrel away	To save	Squirrels collect food in the summer and autumn to eat in the winter.
Weasel words	A statement that seems to have meaning but does not	Weasels are able to suck out the inside of an egg while leaving the shell whole.
Worm	A lowly person	Because worms live in the earth and are slow moving crawlers, they are thought to be inferior animals.

Animal Sounds

There are virtually silent animals, like the stork, but most make sounds. Some of the names given to the cries animals make are listed below.

Apes	gibber	**Frogs**	croak
Bears	growl	**Geese**	cackle
Bees	buzz	**Grasshoppers**	chirp
Birds	sing	**Horses**	neigh
Calves	bleat	**Hyenas**	laugh
Cats	purr	**Lambs**	bleat
Chickens	cackle	**Lions**	roar

Cocks	crow	**Mice**	squeak
Cows	moo	**Monkeys**	chatter
Dogs	bark	**Owls**	hoot
Dolphins	click	**Parrots**	talk
Doves	coo	**Pigs**	grunt
Ducks	quack	**Sheep**	baa
Elephants	trumpet	**Turkeys**	gobble
Fox	yelp	**Wolves**	howl

Animals Who Were First

AARDVARK **'Aardy'** was the first aardvark born in captivity in America. She was born on September 29, 1967, in the Crandon Park Zoo, Miami, Florida. An aardvark is an African mammal that has ears like a donkey's, a tail like a kangaroo's, and a long sticky tongue. It feeds on ants and termites.

CHIMPANZEE **'Washoe'** was the first chimpanzee to learn to communicate in words. She was acquired in 1966 by behavioural psychologists at the University of Nevada in Reno. They taught her the American sign language for the deaf.

DOGS **'Laika'**, a terrier, was the first living space-passenger, when she was launched into orbit in *Sputnik 2* by the Russians on November 3, 1957.

'Buddy', a German sheepdog, was the first dog to be used as a 'seeing eye' for the blind. He was trained by his owner, Morris Eustis, in Switzerland in 1920.

'Rin Tin Tin', a German sheepdog, was the first dog to earn a million dollars. He was a movie 'character' and his first film was *Where the North Begins*, in 1925.

'Rover', a collie, was the world's first dog film star. He appeared in a 1902 movie called *Rescue by Rover*.

GORILLAS

'Koko' was the first gorilla to learn the American sign language for the deaf. Born in July 1971, she was taught by Dr. Franklin Patterson of Stanford University in California.

'Snowflake' was the world's first known albino (white) gorilla. She was discovered in Africa in 1966 and sent to the zoo in Barcelona, Spain.

ELEPHANT

'Jumbo' was the first African elephant to be seen at the London Zoo. He was acquired in 1865 and proved hugely popular with the public. 'Jumbo' was difficult to manage so was eventually sold to Barnum's Circus and toured America as 'The Biggest Animal in Captivity' until a train collided with him and he was killed in 1885.

HORSE

'Red Rum' is the only horse to have won the Grand National Steeplechase three times – in 1973, 1974, and in 1977.

LIGER (half lion, half tiger)

'Shasta' was the first liger born in the United States, She was born on May 6, 1948 at the Hagh Zoo in Salt Lake City, Utah.

MONKEYS

'Able' and **'Baker'** were the first animals to survive being rocketed into space by the United States government. They were sent aloft in a *Jupiter* rocket on May 28, 1959.

GIANT PANDAS

"Ming' and **'Grandma'** were the first Giant Pandas to be seen at the London Zoo when they arrived in December 1938. **'Grandma'** died within a few weeks, but **'Ming'**, who was evacuated to Whipsnade during the war, lived until 1944.

'Yvanjing' was the first Giant Panda bred by artificial insemination. She was born in 1978 in the Beijing Zoo in China.

Migration: Animal Journeys

Migration is a regular, seasonal movement from one part of the world to another by a group of animals. Animals move to find food, a place to breed or a better climate. Mammals migrate in search of food. Fish migrate between fresh and salt water or to different parts of the ocean. Birds usually migrate along regular routes. They are perhaps the most famous migrators. The movement of birds has fascinated scientists, who still don't completely understand how birds find their destinations. Studies have shown that birds use the sun, stars and wind currents to guide them. And yet, birds that have been lost or blown off course are still able to find their homes. Scientists are working to unlock the mysteries of bird and other animal migration. Some of the destinations and distances travelled by animals that are known are listed here.

ANIMAL TRAVELLERS: WHERE AND HOW FAR THEY GO

Flyers

Animal	Distance	Where to and from
Arctic Tern	25,000 miles, round trip	North to South Pole
Cuckoo	8,000 miles, round trip	Europe to North Africa
Stork	15,000 miles, round trip	Mid-Europe to Tropical and South Africa

Swallow	14,000 miles, round trip	Europe to Central and South Africa
Monarch Butterfly	2,000 miles, round trip	Canada to California, USA
	Swimmers	
Atlantic Salmon	4,000 miles, round trip	Northern Europe and North America to Atlantic Ocean
Eel	6,000 miles, round trip	Sargassa Sea to Europe and N. America
Emperor Penguin	1,000–2,000 miles yearly	Antarctica to Weddell Sea
Humpback Whale	8,000 miles, round trip	Indian Ocean to Atlantic Ocean
	Walkers	
Bison	800 miles	Roam the N. Provinces of Canada
Caribou	800 miles	NW Territories of Canada to islands in Arctic Circle
Wildebeest	500 miles	Roam E. Africa

Zoos

COLLECTIONS OF LIVING ANIMALS

From the earliest times, man has been fascinated by animals and their behaviour. Ancient Roman, Egyptian and Chinese emperors all had menageries. These collections of animals were for curiosity or for a show of power. Zoos (zoological gardens) for all people opened in Europe about 200 years ago. Today's zoos are much different from early zoos. They are run for educational, recreational and scientific purposes. They try to provide animals with their natural surroundings. Many hope to preserve rare species by breeding. The following is a list of the oldest and largest zoos in the world and some of the zoos that are noted for recording firsts in zoo history.

OLDEST

EARLIEST KNOWN ZOO
11th century B.C.—Ling-Yu, 'The Garden of Intelligence', was opened in China by the Emperor Wang.

OLDEST EXISTING ZOO IN THE WORLD
1752—The Garden at Schönbrunn, Vienna, Austria.

OLDEST PRIVATELY OWNED ZOO IN THE WORLD
1826—The Zoological Gardens, Regent's Park, London.

OLDEST ZOO IN THE UNITED STATES
1872—The Philadelphia Zoo, Philadelphia, Pennsylvania.

LARGEST

LARGEST ZOO IN THE WORLD (MOST ANIMALS)
The San Diego Wild Animal Park San Diego, California.

LARGEST URBAN (CITY) ZOO IN THE WORLD
New York Zoological Gardens, Bronx, N.Y. covers 252 acres.

FIRSTS

FIRST ZOO IN GREAT BRITAIN was the private zoo of King Henry I at Woodstock Palace. It exhibited foreign wild deer, lions, lynx, a cheetah, a camel, ostriches and a porcupine. It was moved to the Tower of London in the reign of Henry III.

THE FIRST ELEPHANT seen in England was a gift to Henry III from the King of France and was exhibited at the Tower of London.

THE FIRST GIRAFFES seen in England were acquired by George IV in 1827. They were housed in his menagerie at Windsor.

THE FIRST OKAPI was discovered by Europeans in 1899; the first one to be seen in a zoo was in Antwerp, Belgium. The first okapi came to England in 1935.

THE FIRST ZOO DIRECTOR to create a modern 'open' zoo avoiding bars and cages was Carl Hagenbeck, the founder of Hamburg Zoo, in 1900.

THE FIRST DRIVE-THROUGH ANIMAL PARK outside Africa was Longleat Safari Park near Warminster, Wiltshire. Opened in 1966, it covers 360 acres with a 7-mile road system through the separate enclosures. It is famous for its lions.

THE FIRST PÈRE DAVID DEER to come to England from China were acquired by the Duke of Bedford for Woburn Park. Now Woburn Wild Animal Kingdom is the largest drive through Safari Park in Britain and is famous for its collection of deer, including Père David's and the rare Bongo, besides many other species.

THE FIRST LARGE 'OPEN' ZOO in the world opened at Whipsnade near Luton, Bedfordshire in 1931. Comprising 541 acres, enclosed within a six-mile boundary fence, animals live in large groups in spacious paddocks.

EXTINCT AND ENDANGERED ANIMALS

Since the beginning of life, thousands of animal species have come and gone. Extinction (no longer existing) is a natural process. Dinosaurs no longer exist but man had nothing to do with their disappearance. However, in the last few hundred years, the pace of extinction seems to have speeded up. Man has threatened animal life in three main ways: by hunting certain species too much, by polluting the environment through misapplied technology, and by destroying natural animal living space for man's own use.

The International Union for Conservation of Nature and Natural Resources lists 803 species that are in danger of extinction. Some animals such as Przewalski's wild horse and Père David's deer only exist in zoos. Others such as the Arabian oryx and the Hawaiian goose have been saved from extinction by zoos.

Saving animals from extinction is important for man. All life forms are interdependent and the loss of one or two of them can greatly hurt man.

Some experts predict animal extinction at the rate of one a minute by 1990. The following are a few famous examples of animals which no longer exist:

DODO—a large, flightless bird which lived on the islands of Mauritius and Réunion in the Pacific Ocean until it was wiped out on the arrival of man in the early 17th century.
SOLITAIRE—another large, flightless bird which lived on the island of Rodriguez until the 17th century.
QUAGGA—a type of Zebra from Africa which died out at the end of the 19th century.
PASSENGER PIGEON—they thrived in flocks of millions in the U.S.A. but the last survivor was recorded in 1934.
TASMANIAN WOLF—a marsupial wild dog last seen in Hobart in 1934.

The following is a list of some of the world's most endangered animals:

Amphibians

Angonoka tortoise (Madagascar)
Caiman (South America)
Giant tortoise (Galapagos)
Goliath frog (West Africa)
Nile Crocodile (Africa)
Orinoco Crocodile (Venezuela)
Olm Salamander (Adriatic)
Ridge-nosed Rattlesnake (Arizona)
Spade-foot Toad (Italy)

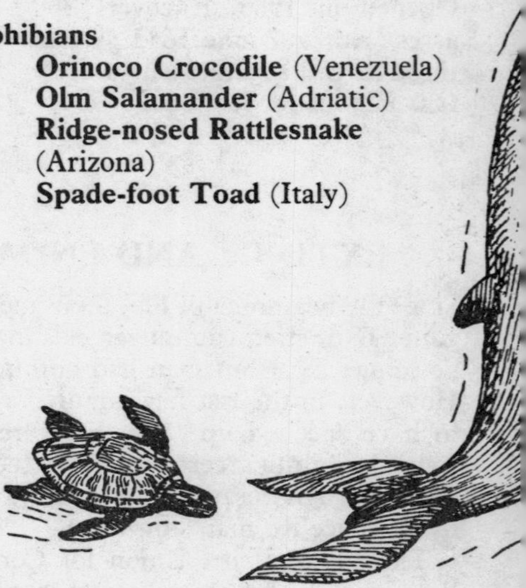

Birds

Condor (California)
Dappled Mountain Robin (E. Africa)
Hermit Ibis (Morocco)
Kagu (New Calidonia, Pacific)
Scarlet Macaw (South America)
Sea Eagle (Scandinavia)

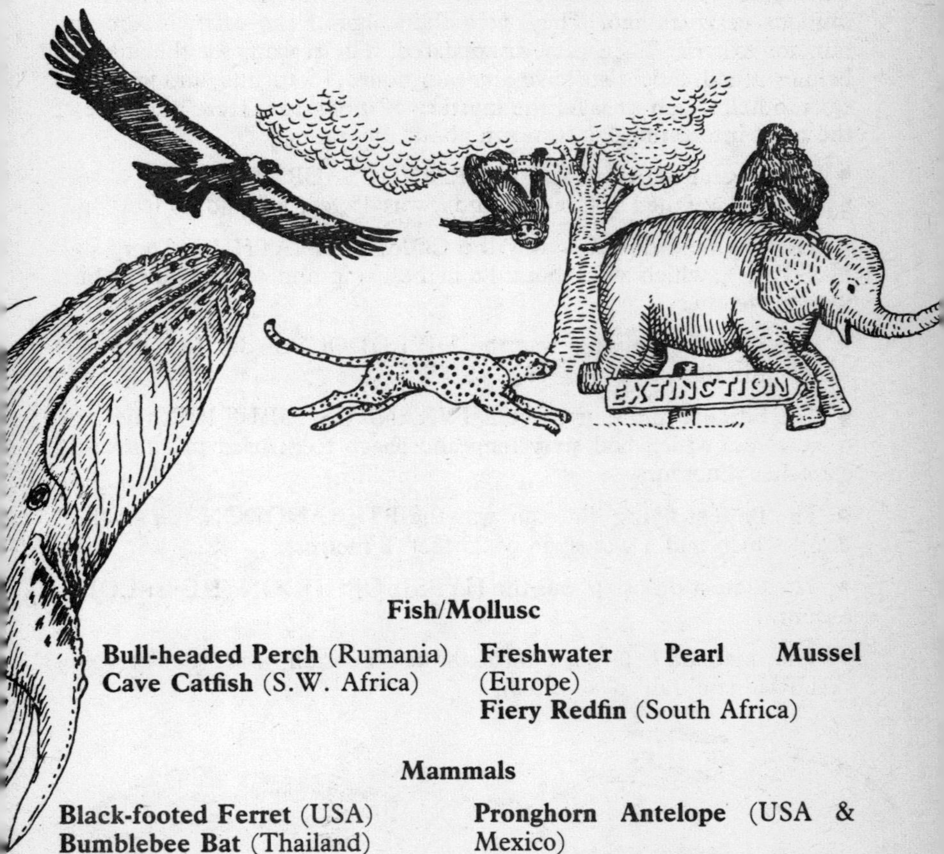

Fish/Mollusc

Bull-headed Perch (Rumania)
Cave Catfish (S.W. Africa)
Freshwater Pearl Mussel (Europe)
Fiery Redfin (South Africa)

Mammals

Black-footed Ferret (USA)
Bumblebee Bat (Thailand)
Giant Otter (Amazon)
Indris (Madagascar)
Jaguar (South America)
Kouprey (Indo-China)
Manatee (Amazon)
Monk Seal (Mediterranean)
Muriqui Monkey (Brazil)
Polar Bear (Arctic)
Pronghorn Antelope (USA & Mexico)
Salt Marsh Harvest Mouse (San Francisco)
Sumatran Rhino (Sumatra)
White Rhinoceros (Central Africa)
Wolf (Arctic)
Woolly Monkey (Andes)

Dinosaurs

Dinosaurs, 'terrible lizards,' were reptiles who lived on the earth millions of years ago. They were the kings of the earth before any humans existed. Then they disappeared. The reasons for this are still being studied. Scientists have dinosaur bones, footprints, and fossilized eggs to help them unravel the mystery of dinosaurs. Here are some of the most interesting facts known about dinosaurs.

- The **largest** dinosaur was the BRACHIOSAURUS (brack' e' o' sore us), which weighed 100,000 pounds, was 45 feet tall and 80 feet long.

- The **smallest** dinosaur was the COMPSOGNATHUS (Comp-sog-Nay-Thus), which was about 12 inches long and looked like a bird without feathers.

- The **longest** dinosaur was the DIPLODOCUS (dip LOD' o cus) which was almost 90 feet long.

- The **fiercest** dinosaur was the TYRANNOSAURUS REX (tie' ran' o' sore' us) which had sixty long and sharp teeth used to attack and eat other dinosaurs.

- The **largest flying** dinosaur was the PTERANODON (ter' AN' o' don), which had a wingspan of 25 feet (8 metres).

- The **fastest** dinosaur was the HYPSILOPHODON (HIP-si-LOFF-o-donn).

- The **last and largest** meat-eating dinosaur was TYRANNO-SAURUS (tie' ran' o' sore' us).

Animal Pets

If you love animals and would like to have one for a pet, there are many things you should consider. When you take a pet into your home, you are responsible for its well-being for a long time.

The following questions will help you decide if you can be a responsible pet owner. They will also help you decide on the best kind of pet for you.

A

	Yes	No
1. Would you love, honour and care for an animal every day for the rest of its life?	☐	☐
2. Could you pay vet's bills for sick- and well-animal care?	☐	☐
3. Would you spay females and neuter males?	☐	☐
4. Are you permitted to have animals where you live?	☐	☐
5. Could you accept an extra three to five pounds tacked onto your housekeeping bill each week?	☐	☐

0–2: Get a pet rock *3–4: Think again* *5: Yes, proceed to Section B*

B

1. Do you live in a house?	☐	☐
2. Do you have an unrestricted choice of the type of animal you may have?	☐	☐
3. Do you have large living quarters?	☐	☐
4. Will someone be home with the animal most of the time?	☐	☐
5. Do you have an area where the animal can be safely exercised on a routine basis?	☐	☐
6. Are you prepared to deal with an animal that may be destructive?	☐	☐
7. Is your family free of allergy problems?	☐	☐
8. Do you travel often?	☐	☐

9. Are you prepared to teach your brothers and sisters how to properly handle an animal? ☐ ☐
10. Do you like to groom animals? ☐ ☐
11. Would you obey lead and path-fouling byelaws? ☐ ☐
12. Do you establish routines and follow them? ☐ ☐
13. Would you laugh if you found fur in your morning cereal? ☐ ☐
14. Can you live in a house that is less than 'hospital clean'? ☐ ☐
15. Do you look forward to getting outside to exercise? ☐ ☐
16. Do you want an animal you can pet and handle? ☐ ☐
17. Do you want an animal that will be a companion? ☐ ☐
18. Would you prefer an animal that needs some care daily to one that needs a lot of care twice a week or weekly? ☐ ☐
19. Do you sleep with the windows open? ☐ ☐
20. Do you prefer a noisy to a quiet living space? ☐ ☐
21. Can you live with stains on your carpet, scratch marks on your chair? ☐ ☐
22. Would you give your pet free access to most areas of the house? ☐ ☐
23. Do you live in a suburban or sparsely populated area? ☐ ☐

0–10: Look into caged animals *11–18: Cat person!*
19–23: Find a breed of dog to match your life-style

Reprinted with permission of *Animals* Magazine

A Partial List of Pets

CAGED ANIMALS: Canaries, gerbils, fish, hamsters, parrots, mice
These animals are totally dependent on you for food, water and a comfortable environment.

CAGED ANIMALS THAT ALSO NEED FREEDOM: Guinea pigs, parakeets, rabbits
These animals depend on you for nourishment and cleaning. When set free, they must be well supervised.

UNCAGED ANIMALS: Cats and dogs
They need food and drink but are able to take care of themselves in many ways. They are the most popular pets because they can adapt to the human life-style.

Books for Children

A treasury of the favourite books of children, classics for all time, and little known facts about books can be found here.

> 'There are more treasures in books than all the pirates' loot in Treasure Island . . . and best of all, you can enjoy these riches every day of your life.'
>
> —WALT DISNEY

Book Bits

*In 300 B.C., Ptolemy I of Egypt founded a great library in Alexandria. The library did not contain books as we know them today—instead, it was filled with scrolls of papyrus. The library, which stood for over 400 years, was considered a cultural wonder of its time.

***The world's first printed book** was the Diamond Sutra. It was printed with wooden blocks and was published in China in 868 A.D.

***The most valuable book in the world** is the Gutenberg Bible which was first printed in 1455, in Mainz, Germany. This bible was the first book ever printed from moveable metal type. It is a huge book with 1,282 sheepskin pages which open to the width of a card table. In 1978 one of the 47 existing copies was sold for $2,400,000. Today, one copy is in the Library of Congress in the U.S., one is in the British Museum in England, and one is in the Biblioteque Nationale in France.

***The first English printer** was William Caxton who printed a translation of *The Recuyell of the Historyes of Troye* in Bruges, Belgium, and a book on chess in 1474. He set up the first printing press in England in Westminster in 1476–77 and his publications included Chaucer's *Canterbury Tales* and Malory's *Le Morte d'Arthur*.

***The first children's book printed in English** was a book of rhymes entitled *A Book in Englyssh Metre of the Great Merchant Man Called Dives Pragmaticus*. It was printed by Alexander Lacy of England in 1563.

***The world's first children's magazine** was published in 1751 by John Newbery of England. The name of the magazine was *The Lilliputian*.

***The British Library** was until 1973 part of the British Museum, which was founded in 1759. It contains books, periodicals, and newspapers in all languages (except those of Asia), maps, musical scores, postage stamps and sound recordings. There are more than 10 million books. 600,000 items are added to the collection annually, requiring nearly 2 miles of additional shelving. The library plans to move to a new building off the Euston Road in London in 1991.

50 Modern Classics for children aged 10 and over

Author	Title
ASHLEY, Bernard	The Trouble With Donovan Croft
BAWDEN, Nina	The Peppermint Pig
BLUME, Judy	Are You There God, It's Me Margaret
BRANFIELD, John	Fox in Winter
BYARS, Betsy	Midnight Fox
CARTER, Peter	The Sentinels
CHRISTOPHER, John	Tripods Trilogy

CLEARY, Beverly	Ramona The Pest
CORMIER, Robert	The Chocolate War
DAHL, Roald	Charlie and The Chocolate Factory
DAVIES, Andrew	Conrad's War
EVANS, Russell	Survival
FARMER, Penelope	Charlotte Sometimes
FITZHUGH, Louise	Nobody's Family is Going to Change
GARDAM, Jane	The Hollow Land
GARFIELD, Leon	John Diamond
GARFIELD, Leon	Smith
GARNER, Alan	The Owl Service
GRANT, Gwen	Private: Keep Out
HARRIS, Rosemary	Zed
HINTON, S.E.	The Outsiders
HOLMAN, Felice	Slake's Limbo
HOY, Linda	Your Friend Rebecca
JONES, Diana Wynne	Magicians Of Caprona
KEMP, Gene	The Turbulent Term of Tyke Tyler
KERR, Judith	When Hitler Stole Pink Rabbit
KING, Clive	Stig of the Dump
KING-SMITH, Dick	Daggie Dogfoot
KONISBERG, E. L.	From the Mixed up Files of Mrs. Basil E. Frankweiler
LE GUIN, Ursula	A Wizard of Earthsea
LEESON, Robert	Bess
LEWIS, C. S.	'Chronicles of Nania' Series
LIVELY, Penelope	The Ghost of Thomas Kempe
MAGORIAN, Michelle	Goodnight Mr. Tom
MARK, Jan	Thunder and Lightenings

McKINLEY, Robin	Beauty
NORTON, Mary	The Borrowers
O'BRIEN, R. C.	Z For Zachariah
PATERSON, Katherine	The Great Gilly Hopkins
RODGERS, Mary	Freaky Friday
TOLKIEN, J. R. R.	The Hobbit
TOWNSEND, John Rowe	Gumble's Yard
TOWNSEND, Sue	The Secret Diary of Adrian Mole Aged 13¾
WALSH, Jill Paton	Gaffer Sampson's Luck
WATSON, J.	Talking in Whispers
WESTALL, Robert	The Machine-Gunners
WHITE, E. B.	Charlotte's Web
WILSON, Jacqueline	Waiting for the Sky to Fall

25 Contemporary Children's Novels which have proved popular for the age 10 and over

Author	Title
ALCOCK, Vivian	The Haunting of Cassie Palmer
BLUME, Judy	Superfudge
BLUME, Judy	Are You There God? It's Me Margaret
BYARS, Betsy	The Eighteenth Emergency
CROSS, Gillian	The Dark Behind The Curtain
DAHL, Roald	The Twits. The Witches. The BFG.

DAVIES, Andrew	Conrad's War
GUY, Rosa	Paris, Peewee and Big Dog
HARRIS, Rosemary	Zed
HOWKER, Janni	The Nature of the Beast
KAYE, Geraldine	Comfort Herself
KING-SMITH, Dick	The Sheep-Pig
LAYTON, George	A Northern Childhood: The Fib and Other Stories
MAGORIEN, Michelle	Goodnight Mr. Tom
MARK, Jan	Handles
MAHY, Margaret	The Changeover
NEEDLE, Jan	A Game of Soldiers
PATON WALSH, Jill	A Parcel of Patterns
PATON WALSH, Jill	Gaffer Sampson's Luck
SWINDELLS, Robert	Brother in the Land
URE, Jean	A Proper Little Nooryeff
WESTALL, Robert	The Scarecrows
WILSON, Jacqueline	The Other Side

Bridges

The first people to live on earth were nomads who moved from place to place looking for food and shelter. They placed fallen trees across streams in order to pass from one side to the other. These trees were the first bridges. As civilization advanced so did the science of bridge building. New materials and techniques were used to build a variety of longer and stronger bridges. Modern man is able to span great bodies of water with spectacular bridges of steel and concrete.

Bridges inspire authors, poets, playwrights, artists, and photographers who praise them in words and pictures. Bridges are among the most complex, beautiful, and endearing structures built.

Major Types of Bridges

FIXED BRIDGES

BEAM

This is the simplest type of bridge. It is constructed by laying beams of wood, steel, or concrete across an expanse. A simple example of this type of bridge is a fallen tree lying across a river with both ends resting on the banks.

CANTILEVER

This bridge is made of three beams. Two beams are anchored to the two sides of the river bank. The third is placed between them to close the gap. Each of the projecting beams is called a cantilever.

SUSPENSION

A suspension bridge is hung from two or more cables which pass over towers and are then anchored on both sides of the crossing. The first suspension bridges were tightropes strung across rivers.

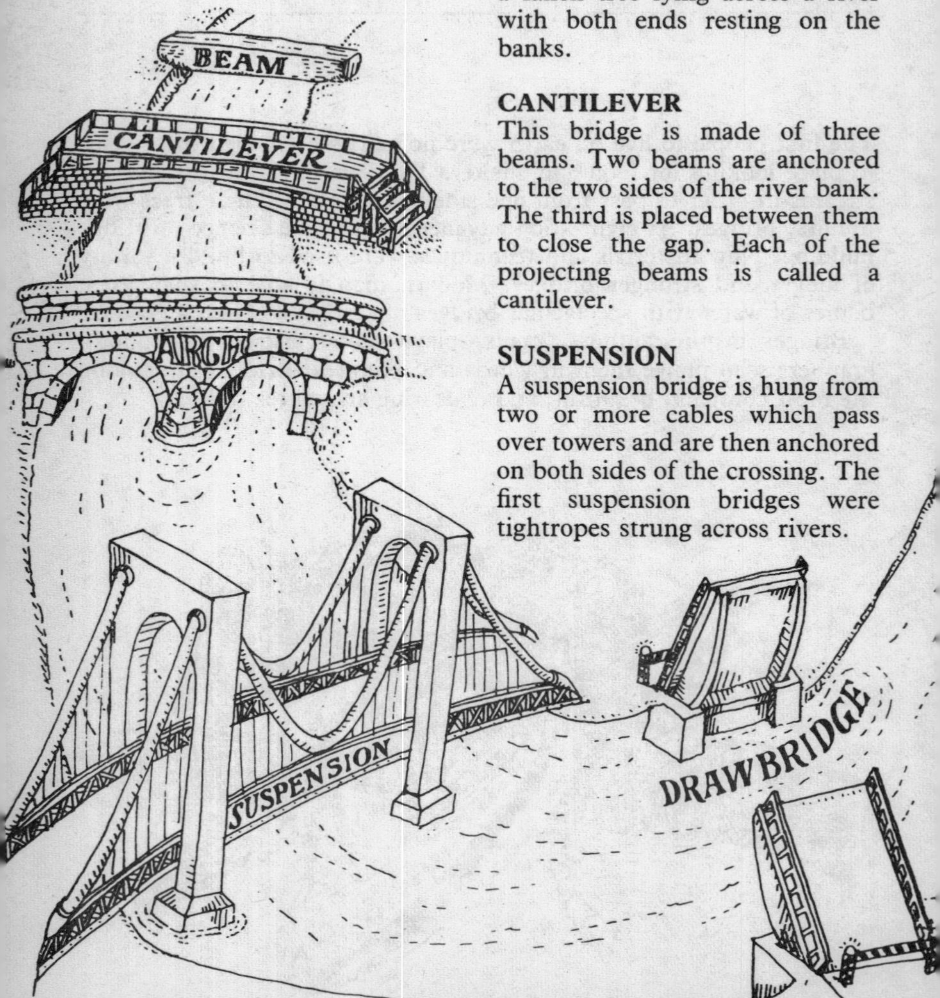

ARCH
An arch bridge curves upward and the ends push outward against a support. It is considered to be an upside-down suspension bridge.

COVERED
This is a wooden bridge with a roof built over it to protect it from rot caused by excessive moisture or dryness.

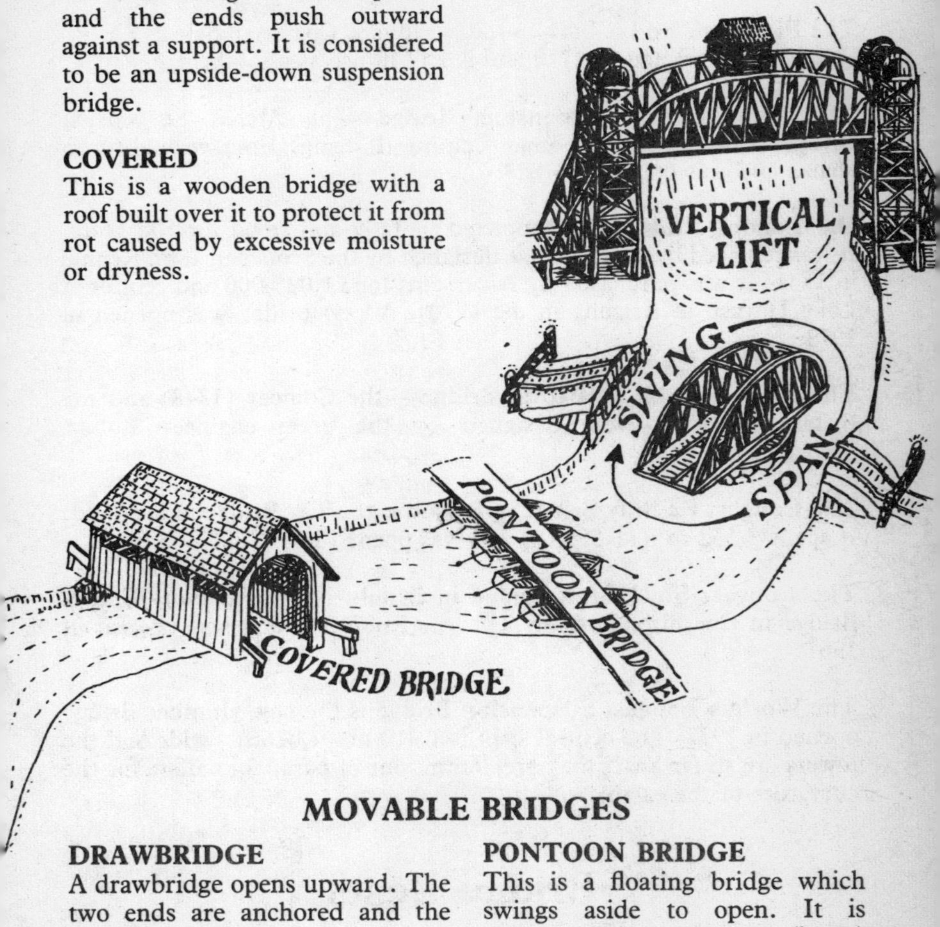

MOVABLE BRIDGES

DRAWBRIDGE
A drawbridge opens upward. The two ends are anchored and the centre swings open.

VERTICAL LIFT
This bridge moves like an elevator. There is a tower at each end of the span and the span is attached to cables which move the bridge up and down.

PONTOON BRIDGE
This is a floating bridge which swings aside to open. It is supported by pontoons (boats) which float on the water.

SWING SPAN
A swing bridge opens outward. It is balanced by a pivot pier which is at its centre.

British Bridges

The First Iron Bridge built in the world is at Coalbrookdale in Shropshire. It was erected in 1779 and is still in use as a footbridge.

The First Great Suspension Bridge—The Menai Suspension Bridge—was built by Thomas Telford. It hangs from wrought-iron chains and was opened in 1823.

Old London Bridge was completed in 1209 and stood for 500 years. It was replaced by a new bridge designed by the Scotsman John Rennie in 1831. It was purchased by Americans for £1,025,000 and rebuilt at Lake Havasu in Arizona in the 1970s. A new bridge was opened in 1973.

The First Tubular Cast-Iron Bridges—the Conway (1848) and the Britannia (1850)—were designed by the great engineer Robert Stephenson.

The Longest Railway Bridge in Britain is the Tay Bridge in Scotland. It spans 3,552 m. (11,653 ft.) and was opened in 1887.

The Longest Steel Arch Bridge in Britain is the Runcorn-Widnes Bridge in Cheshire. It spans 330 m. (1,082 ft.), and was opened in 1961.

The World's Longest Suspension Bridge is the new Humber Bridge opened in 1977. The central span is 1,410 m. (4,626 ft.) wide and the towers are so far apart they are 36mm. out of parallel to allow for the curvature of the earth.

Bridge Bests

COSTLIEST — **The Verrazano-Narrows Bridge** over New York Bay is the most expensive bridge ever built. It was completed in 1964 at a cost of $304,000,000.

MOST FAMOUS — **Old London Bridge**, which spanned the Thames River in England, is considered the most famous bridge in the English-speaking world.

HEAVIEST LOAD CARRYING **Hell Gate Bridge** over the East River in New York City can withstand the heaviest load of traffic. Built in 1917 for railway traffic, it can hold up 24,000 pounds per foot, or a 10,000-ton spread.

HIGHEST **The Royal Gorge Bridge** was built 1,053 feet above the Arkansas River in central Colorado. It is the highest bridge above water in the world.

LONGEST **The Lake Ponchartrain No. 2** in New Orleans, Louisiana, is the world's longest bridge. It is 23.87 miles long. Eight miles of the bridge are out of sight of land. The bridge, which spans Lake Ponchartrain, was completed in 1969.

TALLEST **The Golden Gate Bridge** over San Francisco Bay in San Francisco, California, is the tallest bridge in the world. The towers of this suspension bridge extend 745 feet up above the water.

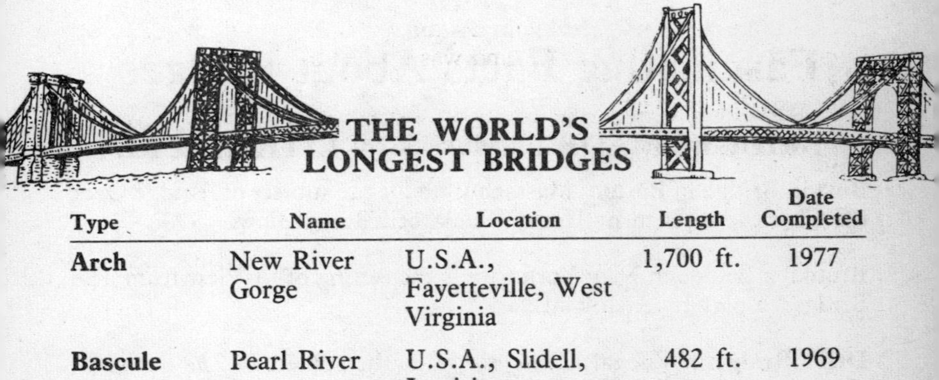

THE WORLD'S LONGEST BRIDGES

Type	Name	Location	Length	Date Completed
Arch	New River Gorge	U.S.A., Fayetteville, West Virginia	1,700 ft.	1977
Bascule	Pearl River	U.S.A., Slidell, Louisianna	482 ft.	1969
Beam	Lake Ponchartrain Number 2	U.S.A., over Lake Ponchartrain, New Orleans, Louisiana	23.87 miles.	1969
Cantilever	Quebec Railway Bridge	Canada, over the St. Lawrence River, Quebec City	3,239 ft	1917

Covered	Hartland Bridge	Canada, New Brunswick Province	1,282 ft.	1899
Pontoon	Evergreen Point Bridge	U.S.A., over Lake Washington, Seattle, Washington	7,518 ft.	1961
Suspension	Humber Bridge	U.K., over the Humber Estuary in Hull, England	4,626 ft.	1977
Swing Span	El Ferdan Bridge	Egypt, over the Suez Canal	552 ft.	1965
Vertical Lift	Arthur Kill Bridge	U.S.A., over the Arthur Channel in Elizabeth, New Jersey	558 ft.	1959

Fascinating Facts About Bridges

BRIDGES MADE FAMOUS IN LITERATURE

Boston Bridge in Boston, Massachusetts, is the subject of 'Bridge Over the Charles,' a poem by Henry Wadsworth Longfellow.

Brooklyn Bridge in New York City is the setting of 'A View from The Bridge,' a play by Arthur Miller.

Drina Bridge in Visegard, Yugoslavia, is the subject of *The Bridge on the Drina*, a Nobel prize-winning novel by Ivo Andue.

Old London Bridge in London, England, is the subject of 'London Bridge Is Falling Down,' a nursery rhyme.

FIVE BRIDGES MADE FAMOUS IN MOVIES

The Bridge of San Luis Rey is a 1945 movie based on a novel of the same name by Thornton Wilder. It is about the collapse of a primitive suspension bridge built by the Inca indians in the Andes mountains of Peru.

The Bridge on the River Kwai is a 1957 movie about a railway bridge built in Siam (now Thailand), by a British colonel captured by the Japanese in World War II.

The Bridge is a 1959 movie about an unnamed bridge defended during World War II by a group of German school boys.

A Bridge Too Far is a 1977 film about the attempt by the 1st Airborne Division to capture the bridge at Arnhem in September 1944, during World War II.

The Bridge at Remagen is a 1969 movie about the bridge across the Rhine River that the allied forces crossed into Germany. The crossing became a turning point in World War II.

FIVE BRIDGES WITH UNUSUAL NAMES

BRIDGE OF BOILS—LIMA, PERU

An epidemic of bubonic plague broke out among the workmen while they were building this bridge. The disease is characterized by boils (made by the swelling of the lymph nodes). The bridge was named Puente de las Verrugus—the Bridge of Boils.

BRIDGE OF SIGHS—VENICE, ITALY

This bridge was named for the sighs of unhappy prisoners who used it to cross from their prison to the palace where they were sentenced for their crimes.

HELL GATE BRIDGE—NEW YORK CITY, U.S.A.
The waters beneath this bridge are so turbulent and treacherous they have been likened to the gates of Hell. Thus, the name Hell Gate Bridge.

HONEYMOON BRIDGE—NIAGARA FALLS, NEW YORK, U.S.A.
This bridge was located in the one-time 'honeymoon capital of America.' Because of the number of married couples who honeymooned in Niagara Falls, the bridge was named the Honeymoon Bridge. It was destroyed in 1938 by an ice jam and replaced by the Rainbow Bridge.

OUTERBRIDGE—STATEN ISLAND, NEW YORK, U.S.A.
It is commonly believed that this bridge was named Outerbridge because of its remoteness from the centre of New York City. It was actually named after Eugenius Outerbridge, the first chairman of New York's Port Authority.

FIVE FAMOUS BRIDGE DISASTERS

TAY BRIDGE OVER THE FIRTH OF TAY, SCOTLAND
On December 28, 1879, the bridge collapsed due to a combination of gale winds and faulty construction. A passenger train with 75 people aboard fell into the water below. There were no survivors.

QUEBEC BRIDGE OVER THE ST. LAURENCE RIVER, QUEBEC CITY, CANADA
On August 29, 1907, while the bridge was under construction, part of it collapsed and 82 workers died.

TACOMA NARROWS BRIDGE OVER PUGET SOUND, TACOMA, WASHINGTON
On November 7, 1940, only four months after this bridge was completed, it collapsed from the force of gale winds. There were no lives lost.

SUNSHINE SKYWAY BRIDGE OVER TAMPA BAY, ST. PETERSBURG, FLORIDA
On May 9, 1980, an ocean freighter smashed into an abutment of the bridge. Three cars, one truck and one bus plummetted into the water. Thirty-five people were killed.

CONNECTICUT TURNPIKE BRIDGE OVER THE MIANUS RIVER, GREENWICH, CONNECTICUT

On June 28, 1983, the bridge collapsed due to disrepair, and three motorists were killed. The collapse of this roadway, an important gateway to New England from New York, resulted in major traffic disruption for months.

FIVE NOTABLE BRITISH BRIDGE BUILDERS

Builder	Bridge	Date Completed
John Rennie (1761–1821)	Tweed Bridge, Kelso	1803
	(Old) Waterloo Bridge, London	1817
	(Old) Southwark Bridge, London	1819
Thomas Telford (1757–1843)	Pont Cysyllte Aqueduct	1805
	Menai Suspension Bridge	1826
	Conway Suspension Bridge	1826
Robert Stephenson (1803–1859)	Conway Tubular Bridge, Caernavonshire	1848
	High Level Bridge, Newcastle	1849
	Britannia Tubular Bridge, Menai Straits	1850

Isambard Kingdom Brunel (1806–1959)	(Old) Charing Cross Bridge, London	1836
	(Old) Hungerford Bridge, London	1845
	Royal Albert Bridge, Saltash, Devon	1859
	Clifton Suspension Bridge, Bristol	1864*
	(*The chains from the demolished Hungerford Bridge were re-used to complete it)	
Gilbert Roberts (1899–1978)	Sydney Harbour Bridge	1932
	Forth Road Bridge	1964
	Severn Suspension Bridge	1966

FIVE CITIES KNOWN FOR THEIR BRIDGES

New York, NY., U.S.A.	1,420 bridges
Sydney, Australia	1,305 bridges
Venice, Italy	450 bridges
Amsterdam, Holland	300 bridges
Osaka, Japan	250 bridges

FIVE BRIDGES PAINTED BY FAMOUS ARTISTS

Pont-Neuf Bridge in Paris, painted by Renoir.
Pont St. Michel Bridge in Paris, painted by Matisse.
The Bridge at Arles, painted by Van Gogh.
Westminster Bridge in London, painted by Monet.
Battersea Bridge in London, painted by Whistler.

Buildings

Just about anywhere there are people, there are buildings. People live, work, play, and pray in buildings. There has always been a close connection between the structures people build and the way they live. The first buildings of primitive people were simple. Through the ages, however, more elaborate and complicated buildings were made. Simple huts, splendid palaces, and towering skyscrapers are all human expressions of beauty, function, and sometimes folly.

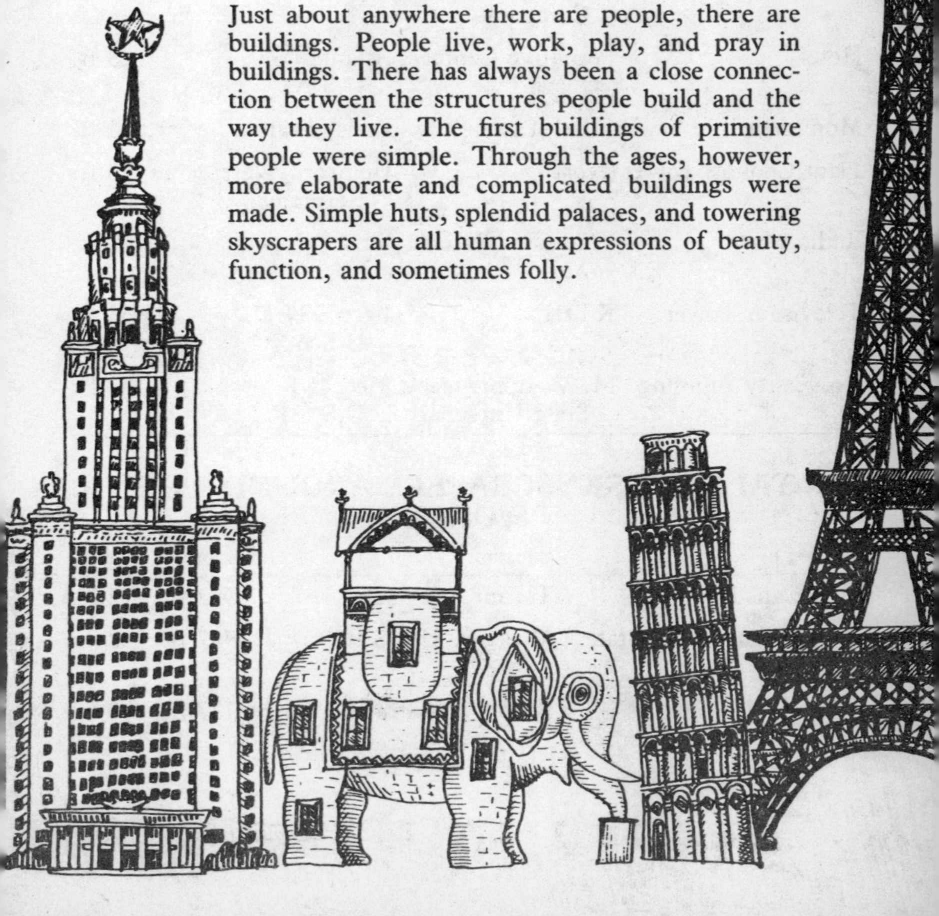

Buildings Bests

THE TALLEST STRUCTURES IN THE WORLD

Type of Structure	Name	Location	Height
Apartment Building	Lake Point Towers	Chicago, Ill., U.S.A.	645 ft.
Cathedral	Ulm	Ulm, West Germany	528 ft.
Factory Chimney	International Nickel Company	Sudbury, Ontario, Canada	1,250 ft.
Hotel	Peachtree Center Plaza	Atlanta, Ga., U.S.A.	723 ft.
Monument	Eiffel Tower	Paris, France	1,052 ft.
Plant Cooling Tower	(*None*)	Uentrop, West Germany	590 ft.
Radio Mast	Warszawa Radio Mast	Plock, Poland	2,121 ft.
Television Tower	KTHI	Fargo, N.D., U.S.A.	2,063 ft.
University Building	M. V. Lomonosov State University	Moscow, U.S.S.R.	787 ft.

TALLEST SKYSCRAPERS AROUND THE WORLD

Building	Location	Height	Stories
First Canadian Place	Toronto, Canada	952 ft.	72
M. V. Lomonosov State University	Moscow, U.S.S.R.	787 ft.	32
Mutual Life Citizens	Sydney, Australia	787 ft.	70

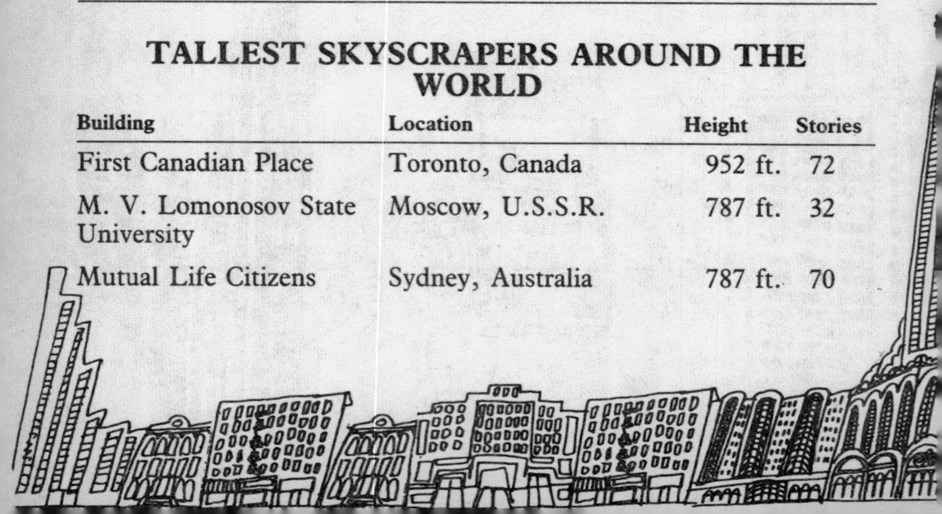

Palace of Science and Culture	Warsaw, Poland	758 ft.	42
Maine Montparnasse	Paris, France	751 ft.	64
Ikebokoru	Tokyo, Japan	741 ft.	60
Carlton Centre	Johannesburg, South Africa	722 ft.	50
Overseas Chinese Banking Corporation	Singapore, Republic of Singapore	660 ft.	52
Parque Central Torre	Caracas, Venezuela	656 ft.	56

THE FIVE TALLEST SKYSCRAPERS IN THE U.S.

Building	Location	Height	Stories
Sears Tower	Chicago, Ill.	1,454 ft.	110
World Trade Center	New York, N.Y.	1,350 ft.	110
Empire State Building	New York, N.Y.	1,250 ft.	102
Standard Oil Building	Chicago, Ill.	1,136 ft.	80
John Hancock Center	Chicago, Ill.	1,127 ft.	100

TALLEST SKYSCRAPERS IN U.S. CITIES

Building	Location	Height	Stories
Texas Commerce Tower	Houston, Tx.	997 ft.	75
First Interstate Bank	Los Angeles, Ca.	858 ft.	62
Transamerica Pyramid	San Francisco, Ca.	853 ft.	48
U.S. Steel Headquarters	Pittsburgh, Penn.	841 ft.	64
John Hancock Tower	Boston, Mass.	790 ft.	60
IDS Tower	Minneapolis, Minn.	775 ft.	57
Peachtree Center Plaza Hotel	Atlanta, Ga.	723 ft.	71

LARGEST BUILDINGS IN THE WORLD

Type of Building	Name	Location	Total Floor Space
Arena	Louisiana Superdome	New Orleans, La., U.S.A.	52 acres
Castle (inhabited)	Windsor Castle	England	51 acres
Church	St. Peter's Basilica	Rome, Italy	162,000 sq. ft.
Department Store	Macy's	New York, N.Y., U.S.A.	50 acres
Hotel	Waldorf Astoria	New York, N.Y., U.S.A.	1,900 rooms
Housing Complex	Co-op City	Bronx, N.Y., U.S.A.	15,000 apartments (1,350 acres)
Industrial Plant	Nizhnigtagil Railroad Car & Tank Plant	U.S.S.R.	204.3 acres
Office Building	The Pentagon	Washington, D.C., U.S.A.	6,500,000 sq. ft.
Opera House	Metropolitan Opera House	New York, N.Y.	3,800 sq. ft.

Private House	The Biltmore House	Asherville, N.C., U.S.A.	250 rooms
Museum	Museum of Natural History	New York, N.Y., U.S.A.	23 acres
Synagogue	Temple Emanu-el	New York, N.Y.	24,000 sq. ft.
Theatre	National People's	Peking, China	12.9 acres
Toy shop	Hamleys	London, England	45,000 sq. ft.

Official Homes for Heads of Government

Country	Name of Home	Head of Government	Location
Australia	The Lodge	Prime Minister	Canberra, Australia
Belgium	Chateau de Lachen	King	Brussels, Belgium
France	L'Élysée Palace	President	Paris, France
Italy	Quiranale	President	Rome, Italy
Mexico	Los Pinos	President	Mexico City, Mexico
Portugal	Palacio de Belem	President	Lisbon, Portugal
Spain	Palacio de la Moncloe	Premier	Madrid, Spain
West Germany	Federal Chancellor's Office	Chancellor	Bonn, West Germany
United Kingdom	10 Downing Street	Prime Minister	London, England
United States	The White House	President	Washington, D.C., USA

Seven Wonders of the Ancient World

Name	Type of Structure	Location	Remains
The Pyramids	Tombs	El Giza, Egypt	Still standing.
Hanging Gardens of Babylon	Monument	Babylon, Iraq	No ruins remain.
Statue of Zeus	Statue	Olympia, Greece	All traces of it are lost, except for reproductions on coins.
Temple of Diana at Ephesus	Temple	Ephesus, Greece (Modern Turkey)	Destroyed by the Goths in A.D. 262.
Mausoleum at Halicarnassus	Tomb	Bodrum, Turkey	Destroyed by an earthquake in the Middle Ages.

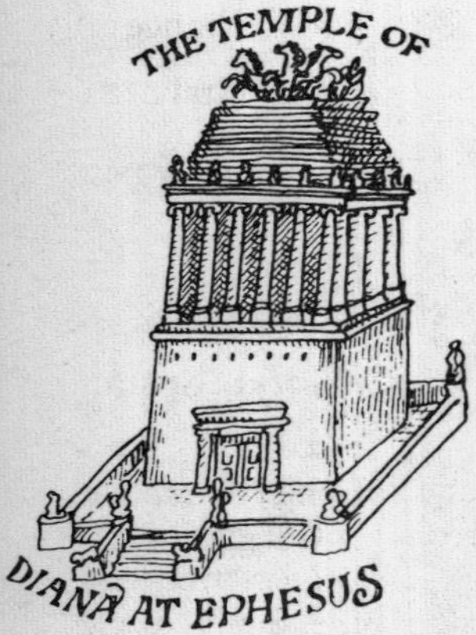

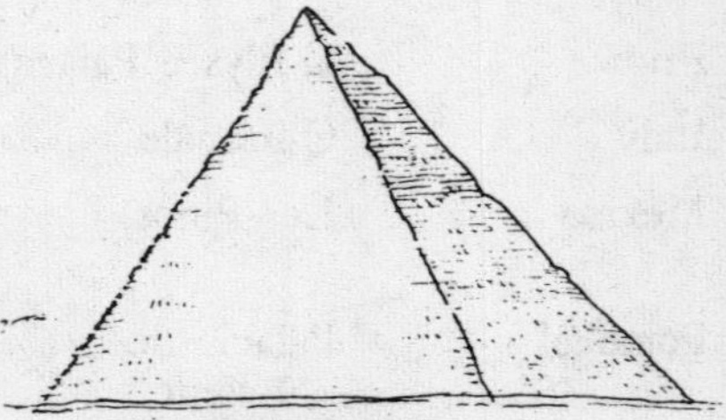
THE PYRAMIDS

THE LIGHTHOUSE AT PHAROS

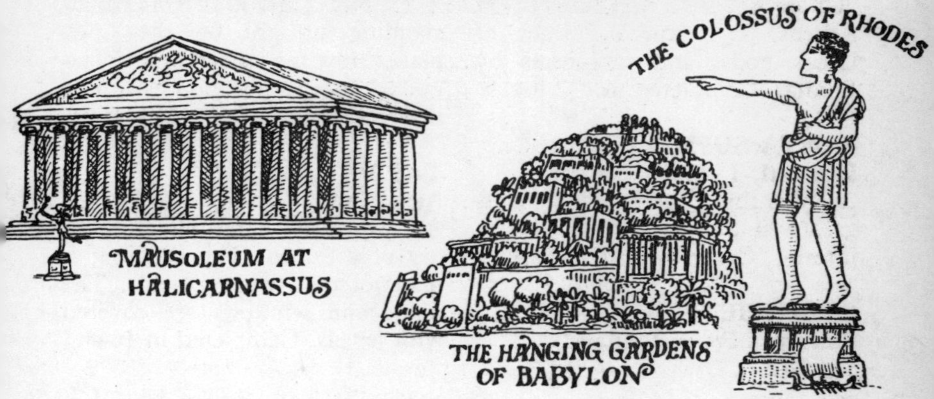

Colossus of Rhodes	Statue	Rhodes, Greece	Destroyed by an earthquake in 224 B.C.
Lighthouse at Pharos	Monument	Alexandria, Egypt	Destroyed by an earthquake in the 13th century.

Seven Other Wonders of the World

COLOSSEUM
Rome, Italy
A giant-sized open theatre with a network of arches, vaulted tunnels and stairways with seating for thousands of spectators. Completed in 80 A.D.

GREAT WALL OF CHINA
China
A 1,500-mile wall built of stone, brick, and earth to safeguard the country. The colossal effort it took to build the wall is equal to the labour of a million people working 25 years.

LEANING TOWER OF PISA
Pisa, Italy
An eight-story bell tower with a winding staircase and picturesque marble inlays. The entire building tilts as a result of repeated earth tremors.

PARTHENON
Athens, Greece
A temple built on the Acropolis,

200 feet above the streets of Athens. It featured statues of Greek gods, and sculptures by Phidias. Completed in 432 B.C.

SANTA SOPHIA
Istanbul, Turkey
A Byzantine church noted for its great gold dome and lavish interior. Completed in 537 A.D.

STONEHENGE
Salisbury Plain, England
A group of massive stones standing upright on the open plain. How the stones were transported to this location is still a mystery. Built around 2400 B.C.

TAJ MAHAL
Agra, India
An exquisite tomb built in memory of a queen. The building is made of pure white marble. The doors and windows are covered with jewels. Completed in 1648.

Notable Homes

TEN SPLENDID HOMES

BRIGHTON PAVILION
Brighton, England
Built for George IV, Prince Regent, by the architect, John Nash. The entire house is of oriental design and features a lavish dining hall and kitchen. Completed 1815.

CHATEAU OF CHAMBORD
Loire Valley, France
Built by King Francois I. A holiday home consisting of 440 rooms, 350 chimneys, and 75 staircases, built on 14,000 acres of gardens surrounded by a 20-mile wall. Completed 1534.

HADRIAN'S VILLA
Tivoli, Italy
Built by Emperor Hadrian. This villa included 7 square miles of buildings and gardens enclosed by a wall. A house, theatre, library, and baths were among the buildings set in lovely gardens of trees and flowers. Completed 124 A.D.

MONTICELLO
Charlottesville, Virginia, U.S.A.
Built by Thomas Jefferson. Thomas Jefferson designed this house which rests on a little mountain (*monticello* in Italian) situated on 5,000 acres of land. The house features a dumbwaiter for bringing wines up from the cellar, and a special passageway for the removal of chamber pots. Completed 1772.

PALACE OF ALHAMBRA
Granada, Spain
Built by Ibnal Ahmar, the Sultan of Granada. The floor space of this unique palace encompasses 9 acres. The sounds of running water can be heard in every palace room. The house was designed to funnel a natural stream through fountains, and reflecting pools were built into all of the rooms. Completed 1358.

SAN SIMEON CASTLE
San Simeon, California, U.S.A.
Built by William Randolph Hearst. It cost $50 million to build this estate overlooking the Pacific Ocean. It is located on 240,000 acres of land and boasts a house with elevators, pools, movie rooms, and dining halls. Completed 1925.

SAN SOUCI
Cap Haitien, Haiti
Built by King Henry Christopher. This huge house was built over a mountain stream so that the lower floors would be cooled by running water. The rooms are decorated with lavish paintings and furniture imported from Europe. The

floors are made of marble and mahogany. Completed 1813.

THE BREAKERS
Newport, Rhode Island, U.S.A.
Built by Cornelius Vanderbilt II. This is a 70-room fireproof 'summer cottage' built at a cost of $10 million. The elaborate interior includes carved pillars and gold trimmed walls. Sixty overnight guests could be accommodated at one time. It is now a museum. Completed 1895.

THE PALACE OF VERSAILLES
Versailles, France
Built by King Louis XIV. It took 36,000 men some 50 years to build it. The Palace has splendid suites of rooms, private salons, banquet halls and ballrooms. The Hall of Mirrors, and lavish gardens are among its outstanding features. Completed 1705.

XANADU
Orlando, Florida, U.S.A.
Built by Roy E. Mason. This house was built to be 'The Home of the Future.' It is constructed of multiple domes made of plastic foam. It provides all the comforts of modern technology, including video monitoring and a computerized kitchen. Completed 1983.

NINE UNUSUAL HOMES

ELEPHANT HOUSE
Margate, New Jersey
Built by James Lafferty. This is an 8-room house built of wood and coated with tin. This 90-ton house is shaped like an elephant. Completed 1881.

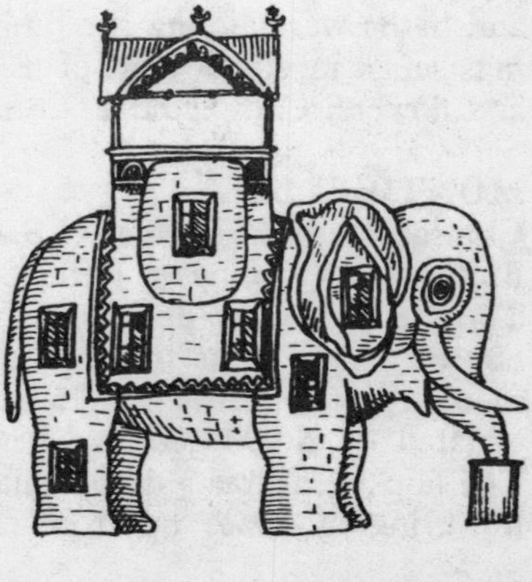

GHOST-PROOF MANSION
San Jose, California
Built by Sarah Winchester. This is a 750-room house designed to fool ghosts. Rooms were built, then torn down over a 38-year period. Fake chimneys, doors, and staircases which lead to blank walls are among its curiosities. Completed 1922.

GLASS HOUSE
New Canaan, Connecticut
Built by Philip Johnson. This is an all-glass rectangular-shaped house. Thin columns of steel support the roof. There are no rooms inside but cabinets are lined up to divide living areas. Completed 1949.

HOUSE ON THE ROCK
Spring Green, Wisconsin
Built by Alex Jordan. This house sits on a sixty-foot-high rock overlooking a valley four hundred and fifty feet below. Five hundred tons of mortar and five thousand tons of stone were used in the house; some transported to the top of the rock by electric hoists, some carried up by Alex Jordan. Completed 1960.

PAPER HOUSE
Pigeon Cove, Massachusetts
Built by Elis F. Stenman. Approximately 100,000 newspapers were used to construct this house and the furniture within it. The walls were made of layers of pasted and folded newspapers. Papers rolled into different sizes make up the furniture which includes tables, chairs, lamps, and a grandfather clock. Completed 1942.

HOUSE OF BOTTLES
British Columbia, Canada
Built by George Plumb. The entire house is constructed of 18,000 liquor, soda, medicine, and beer bottles. Completed 1978.

PRAIRIE CHICKEN
Norman, Oklahoma
Built by Herbert Green. This house, built in the shape of a chicken, is made of wooden planks and corrugated metal. Completed 1962.

REVOLVING HOUSE
Wilton, Connecticut
Built by Richard Foster. This is a circular-shaped house with rooms shaped like slices of a pie. The house rests on a 3-ton ball bearing and revolves by the power of a 1½ h.p. motor. Completed 1968.

UNDERGROUND HOUSE
Fresno, California
Built by Forestiere Baldasera. This 90-room house was dug under the earth by the owner. It took 44 years to complete but cost only $300. Completed 1946.

A Calendar for Children

365 DAYS OF WORLDWIDE EVENTS, HOLIDAYS AND BIRTHDAYS

In many countries of the world almanacs were the first books published. These almanacs always included a calendar—a guide to the passing of time.

Although calendars seem very simple, it took many centuries for calendars to evolve as we know them today. This calendar lists a year of worldwide events, holidays and birthdays. You'll find interesting anniversaries for every day of the year.

Key to Symbols

★ Holidays **◇ Events** **◆ Birthdays** **● Deaths**

January

FLOWER: CARNATION
BIRTHSTONE: GARNET

1

★ New Year's Day.
● James Stuart, the Old Pretender, died 1766.
◇ Queen Victoria proclaimed Empress of India, 1887.

2

◇ Luna I, the first rocket to pass near the moon, launched 1959.

3

◆ J.R.R. Tolkien, author of *The Hobbit* and *The Lord of the Rings*, born 1892.
● William Joyce ('Lord Haw-Haw') executed as a traitor, 1946.

4
◆ Sir Isaac Newton, scientist and mathematician, born 1643.
◆ Jacob Grimm, German author of *Grimm's Fairy Tales* (with his brother Wilhelm), born 1745.
● Louis Braille, the inventor of Braille alphabet for the blind, died 1809.

5
● Edward the Confessor died 1066.
● Sir Ernest Shackleton, explorer, died 1922.

6
◆ Richard II born 1367.
◆ Joan of Arc born c. 1412.
◆ Jacques Montgolfier, balloonist, born 1745.
◇ First round-the-world commercial airline flight by Pan-American airlines, 1942.

7
● Catherine of Aragon, first wife of Henry VIII, died 1536.

8
● Galileo, Italian astronomer, died 1642.
◆ Elvis Presley, singer, born 1935.
● Lord Baden-Powell, founder of the Boy Scouts, died 1941.

9
● Katherine Mansfield, novelist, died 1923.

10
◇ Penny Post started in Britain 1840.
◇ London's Underground Railway opened 1863.
● William Frederick Cody ('Buffalo Bill') died 1917.

11
● Agatha Christie, crime writer, died 1976.

12
● Neville Shute, novelist, died 1960.

13
● James Joyce, novelist, died 1941.

14
● Edmund Halley, astronomer, died 1742.
◆ Albert Schweitzer, medical missionary, born 1875.
● Lewis Carroll ('Charles Dodgson'), author *Alice's Adventures in Wonderland*, died 1898.

15
◆ Maza de la Roche, author of *Whiteoaks* series of books, born 1885.
◆ Martin Luther King, Civil Rights Leader, born 1929.

16
● Edmund Spenser, poet, died 1599.
◇ Shackleton's expedition reached Magnetic South Pole, 1909.

17
◆ Benjamin Franklin, American statesman and inventor, born 1706.
◇ Battle of Falkirk, 1746.
◇ US launched first atomic-powered submarine, the U.S.S. *Nautilus*, 1954.

18
◆ A. A. Milne, author of *Winnie the Pooh*, born 1882.
◇ Captain Scott reached the South Pole, 1912.

19
◆ James Watt, Scottish inventor, born 1736.
◆ Edgar Allan Poe, writer of macabre stories, born 1809.
◆ Paul Cézanne, French artist, born 1839.

20
● George V died 1936.

21
● George Orwell (Eric Blair), author of *1984* and *Animal Farm*, died 1950.
● Cecil B. de Mille, film producer, died 1959.

22
◆ Lord Byron, poet, born 1788.
● Queen Victoria died 1901.

23
◆ Edouard Manet, French artist, born 1832.
● Charles Kingsley, author of *Westward Ho*! and *Hereward the Wake*, died 1875.
● Sir Alexander Korda, film producer, died 1956.

24
◆ Sir John Vanbrugh, dramatist and architect of Blenheim Palace, born 1664.
◆ William Congreve, dramatist, born 1670.
● Sir Winston Churchill, statesman, died 1965.

25
◆ Robert Boyle, physicist, born 1627.
◆ Robert Burns, Scottish poet and author of 'Auld Lang Syne', born 1759.

26
● Edward Jenner, pioneer of vaccination, died 1823.
● W. B. Yeats, Irish poet, died 1939.

27
◆ Wolfgang Amadeus Mozart, Austrian composer, born 1756.
◆ Lewis Carroll (Charles Dodgson) born 1832.
◇ John Logie Baird gave first public demonstration of television in Britain, 1926.

28

● Sir Francis Drake, the greatest of the Elizabethan seamen, died in Panama 1596.

● W. B. Yeats, Irish poet and dramatist, died 1939.

29

◇ Victoria Cross instituted 1856.

◆ Anton Chekhov, Russian playwright, born 1860.

30

● Charles I executed in Whitehall 1647.

● Orville Wright, pioneer of aviation, died 1948.

● Mahatma Gandhi, Indian leader, assassinated 1948.

31

● Guy Fawkes hanged, drawn and quartered 1606.

● Charles Edward Stuart, the Young Pretender, died in Rome 1788.

◇ Brunel's *The Great Eastern* launched 1858.

● A. A. Milne, creator of *Christopher Robin*, died 1956.

February

FLOWER: VIOLET
BIRTHSTONE: AMETHYST

1

● Buster Keaton, film actor, died 1966.

2

Candlemas.

◆ James Joyce, Irish writer, born 1882.

3

◆ Felix Mendelssohn born 1809.

● Boris Karloff, film actor, died 1969.

4

◆ Charles Lindbergh, who made the first non-stop Transatlantic flight in 1927, born 1902.

5

◆ John Boyd Dunlop, the Scottish inventor of the pneumatic tyre, born 1840.

6

◇ Queen Elizabeth II succeeded to the throne, 1952.

7

◆ Charles Dickens, author of *Oliver Twist* and *Great Expectations*, born 1812.

8

● Mary, Queen of Scots, executed 1587.

◆ Jules Verne, French science fiction writer, born 1828.

9

● Lord Darnley, husband of Mary, Queen of Scots, murdered 1567.

◆ Anthony Hope, author of *The Prisoner of Zenda*, born 1863.

10

◆ Boris Pasternak, Russian writer and author of *Doctor Zhivago*, born 1890.

● Lord (Joseph) Lister, pioneer of antisepsis, died 1912.

11

◆ William Fox Talbot, pioneer photographer, born 1800.

◆ Thomas Edison, American inventor, born 1847.

● John Buchan, author of *The Thirty-nine Steps*, died 1940.

◇ First Miracle of Lourdes 1858.

12

● Lady Jane Grey, Queen of England July 9 – 19, executed 1567.

◆ Charles Darwin born 1809.

◇ Alexander Selkirk, the real-life 'Robinson Crusoe', rescued 1709.

13

● Catherine Howard, fifth wife of King Henry VIII, executed 1542.

◇ The massacre of the Macdonalds at Glencoe, 1692.

14

St. Valentine's Day.

● Captain James Cook, navigator and explorer, murdered in Hawaii, 1779.

● P. G. Wodehouse, creator of the *Bertie Wooster* and *Jeeves* stories, died 1975.

15

◆ Galileo, Italian astronomer and physicist, born 1564.

◇ Britain officially adopted decimal currency, 1971.

16

◆ Giambattista Bodoni, Italian printer, born 1740.

17

● Molière, French playwright, died 1673.

18

◆ Mary I, Queen of England 1553 – 58, born 1516.

◆ Volta, Italian inventor of the electric battery, born 1745.

● Michelangelo, Italian painter, died 1546.

19

◆ David Garrick, British actor, born 1717.

● Charles Blondin, who first

crossed Niagara on a tight-rope in 1859, died 1897.

20

● James I, King of Scotland, assassinated 1437.

◇ John Glenn became the first U.S. astronaut to orbit the Earth in 1962.

21

◆ W. H. Auden, poet, born 1907.

22

◆ George Washington, first President of the USA, born 1732.

◆ Robert Baden-Powell, founder of the Boy Scout movement, born 1857.

23

◆ Samuel Pepys, diarist, born 1633.

◆ George Frederick Handel, composer, born 1685.

● Sir Joshua Reynolds, painter, died 1792.

● John Keats, poet, died 1821.

24

● Robert Fulton, American pioneer of steamboats, died 1815.

25

● Sir Christopher Wren, architect, died 1723.

◆ Pierre Auguste Renoir, French Impressionist artist, born 1841.

● Sir John Tenniel, illustrator of *Alice's Adventures in Wonderland*, died 1914.

26

◆ Victor Hugo, French writer, born 1802.

◆ William F. Cody, 'Buffalo Bill', born 1846.

27

◆ Constantine the Great, Roman Emperor 312 – 337, born 280(?)

28

◆ Stephen Spender, poet, born 1909.

● Henry James, American novelist, died 1916.

March

FLOWER: DAFFODIL
BIRTHSTONE: AQUAMARINE

1

◆ Frederic Chopin, composer, born 1810.

◆ Augustus Pugin, architect, born 1812.

2

● John Wesley, founder of Methodism, died 1791.

● D. H. Lawrence, novelist, died 1930.

◆ Dr. Seuss (Theodore Geisel), American author of *The Cat in the Hat* and *The Grinch who Stole Christmas*, born 1904.

3

● Robert Adam, architect, died 1792.

◆ Alexander Graham Bell, Scottish-American inventor, born 1847.

4

◆ Henry the Navigator, Portuguese prince, born 1394.

◆ Antonio Vivaldi, Venetian composer, born 1678.

5

◆ Gerhardus Mercator, Flemish map maker, born 1512.

● Flora Macdonald, Scottish heroine, died 1790.

● Joseph Stalin, Russian leader, died 1953.

6

◆ Michelangelo, Italian artist, born 1475.

● Louisa M. Alcott, American author of *Little Women*, died 1888.

7

◆ William Wordsworth, poet, born 1770.

◆ Sir John Herschel, astronomer, born 1792.

8

◆ Kenneth Grahame, author of *Wind in the Willows*, born 1859.

9

◆ William Cobbett, pamphleteer and author of *Rural Rides*, born 1763.

10

◇ The Bakerloo Line of the London Underground opened 1906.

11

◆ Malcolm Campbell, holder of world speed records on land and water, born 1885.

● Sir Alexander Fleming, discoverer of penicillin, died 1955.

12

◆ Thomas Arne, composer of 'Rule Britannia', born 1710.

13

● Richard Burbage, actor, colleague of William Shakespeare and the builder of the Globe Theatre, died 1619.

◇ The planet Uranus discovered by Sir William Herschel 1781.

14

◆ Albert Einstein, the physicist who developed theories of relativity, born 1879.

● Karl Marx, political philosopher, died 1883.

◇ First transatlantic broadcast made 1925.

15

● Julius Caesar assassinated 44BC.

◇ Selfridge opened in London 1909.

16

◆ George Ohm, physicist, born 1787.

17

★ St. Patrick's Day.

◆ Kate Greenaway, illustrator of children's books, born 1849.

18

◆ Rudolf Diesel, German inventor of the diesel engine, born 1858.

◇ Alexei Leonov, Russian astronaut, was the first person to walk in space, 1965.

19

◆ David Livingstone, missionary explorer, born 1813.

◇ The Tolpuddle Martyrs sentenced to deportation, 1834.

◇ Sydney Harbour Bridge officially opened 1932.

● Edgar Rice Burroughs, creator of *Tarzan*, died 1950.

20

● Sir Isaac Newton, scientist and mathematician, died 1727.

21

● Thomas Cranmer, Archbishop of Canterbury 1533 – 56, burned at the stake, Oxford 1556.

◇ The Sharpeville Massacre, South Africa, 1960.

22

◆ Anthony Van Dyke, Flemish portrait painter, born 1599.

23

◇ The first official settlers landed at Dunedin, New Zealand, 1848.

24

● Queen Elizabeth I, died at Richmond, Surrey 1603.

◆ William Morris, craftsman, poet and reformer, born 1843.

25

Lady Day, which until 1752 was the legal beginning of the year.

◆ Bela Bartok, Hungarian composer, born 1881.

26

● Sir John Vanbrugh, dramatist and architect, died 1726.

● Ludwig van Beethoven, composer, died 1827.

◆ A. E. Housman, author of the poem *The Shropshire Lad*, born 1859.

◆ Tennessee Williams, American playwright, born 1911.

● Sir Noel Coward, actor, dramatist and composer of light music, died 1973.

27

◆ Wilhelm von Rontgen, discoverer of X-rays, born 1845.

28

◆ Raphael, Italian artist, born 1483.

● President Eisenhower, soldier and statesman, died 1969.

29

◆ Sir Edwin Lutyens, architect, born 1869.

◇ Captain R. F. Scott, made his last entry in his diary '. . . the end cannot be far', 1912.

30

◆ Francisco de Goya, Spanish painter, born 1746.

◆ Vincent Van Gogh, Dutch Post-Impressionist painter, born 1853.

◆ Sean O'Casey, Irish playwright, born 1880.

31

◆ Franz Joseph Hayden, Austrian composer, born 1732.

● John Constable, English painter, died 1837.

● Charlotte Bronte, author of *Jane Eyre*, died 1855.

◇ Eiffel Tower in Paris officially opened 1889.

April

FLOWER: SWEET PEA
BIRTHSTONE: DIAMOND

1

April Fools' Day.
◆ William Harvey, discoverer of the circulation of the blood, born 1578.

2

◆ Hans Christian Andersen, Danish story-teller, born 1805.
● C. S. Forester, creator of '*Hornblower*', died 1966.

3

● Johannes Brahms, German composer, died 1897.

4

◆ Grinling Gibbons, English sculptor and wood carver, born 1648.
● Martin Luther King, American Civil Rights leader, assassinated in Memphis, Tennessee, 1968.

5

◆ Joseph Lister, pioneer of antisepsis, born 1827.

6

● King Richard I 'Coeur de Lion' killed in battle at Chaluz, France, 1199.
● Raphael, Italian artist, died 1520.
◇ First modern Olympic Games held in Athens, 1896.

7

● William Wordsworth, poet, died 1770.
● Henry Ford, pioneer motor manufacturer, died 1947.

8

● El Greco, Spanish painter, died 1614.

● Pablo Picasso, Spanish-born painter and a pioneer of Cubism, died 1973.

9

◆ Isambard Kingdom Brunel, great British engineer, born 1806.

● Dante Gabriel Rosetti, poet, painter and a founder of the pre-Raphaelite Brotherhood, died 1882.

10

● Auguste Lumière who, together with his brother Louis Jean, invented a ciné camera and a process of colour photography, died 1954.

11

◇ American Civil War began 1861.

12

● William Kent, architect, died 1748.

● Franklin D. Roosevelt, President of USA 1933–45, died 1945.

◇ USSR launched the first man into space, Yuri Gagarin, 1961.

13

◆ Richard Trevithick, Cornish engineer and pioneer of railway locomotives, born 1771.

14

● Abraham Lincoln, American President, shot at Ford's Theatre, Washington. He died on the 15th, 1865.

◇ *S.S. Titanic* sank on her maiden voyage (night of 14/15) after striking an iceberg, 1912.

15

◆ Leonardo da Vinci, Italian artist, scientist and inventor, born 1452.

16

◆ Sir John Franklin, English explorer, born 1784.

◆ Sir Charles Chaplin, the comic genius of the movies, born 1889.

17

◆ Sir Leonard Woolley, English archaeologist, born 1880.

◆ Benjamin Franklin, American printer and inventor, born 1790.

18

● Albert Einstein, one of the greatest mathematical physicists of all time and world famous for his Theories of Relativity, died 1921.

19

● Lord Byron, English poet, died at Missolonghi, Greece, 1824.

20

● Canaletto, Venetian painter, died 1768.

◆ Adolf Hitler, German Nazi Dictator, born 1889.

21

◆ Charlotte Brontë, author of *Jane Eyre*, born 1816.

● Samuel Clemens ('Mark Twain') author of *Tom Sawyer* and *Huckleberry Finn*, died 1910.

22

◆ Henry Fielding, English novelist, born 1707.

● Richard Trevithick, pioneer of steam engines, died 1833.

23

St. George's Day, Patron Saint of England.

◆● William Shakespeare born (traditional date) at Stratford-upon-Avon 1564, and died there 1616.

◆ J. M. W. Turner, English landscapes painter, born 1775.

● William Wordsworth, poet, died 1850.

● Rupert Brooke, poet, died in Greece, 1915.

24

● Duchess of Windsor, widow of Edward VIII, died 1986.

25

Anzac Day, commemorating the landing of Australia and New Zealand forces at Gallipoli in 1915.

◆ Oliver Cromwell born 1599.

● Guglielmo Marconi, Italian inventor of the radio, died 1874.

26

● Daniel Defoe, author of *Robinson Crusoe*, died 1731.

◆ John James Audubon, American ornithologist, born 1785.

27

◆ Samuel Morse, inventor of Morse Code, born 1791.

28

● Benito Mussolini, Italian Fascist dictator, executed 1945.

29

◆ Duke of Wellington born 1769.

◇ Botany Bay, Australia, discovered by Captain Cook, 1770.

30

● Wilbur Wright, American pioneer aviator, died 1912.

● Adolf Hitler, German Nazi Dictator, committed suicide, 1945.

May

FLOWER: LILY OF THE VALLEY
BIRTHSTONE: EMERALD

1

May Day.
◆ Duke of Wellington, victor of the Battle of Waterloo, born 1769.
● David Livingstone, Scottish missionary and explorer, died 1873.

2

● Leonardo da Vinci, Italian painter, sculptor, architect and engineer, died 1519.
◆ Jerome K. Jerome, English author of *Three Men in a Boat*, born 1859.

3

◆ Nicolo Machiavelli, whose writings gave rise to the word 'machiaevellian' as the embodiment of evil, born 1469.

4

◇ The Battle of Tewkesbury, 1471.

5

◆ Karl Marx, author of *Des Kapital*, born 1818.

6

◆ Sigmund Freud, the Austrian founder of 'psychoanalysis', born 1856.
◇ Sir Roger Bannister ran the first '4 minute mile' in 3 min. 59. 4 sec. in 1954.

7

◆ Johannes Brahms, German composer, born 1833.
◆ Peter Ilyich Tchaikovsky, Russian composer, born 1840.
◇ The *Lusitania*, a British passenger ship, was sunk by a German U-boat, which was one factor that brought America into the war, 1915.

8

◇ VE Day (Victory in Europe) 1945.
● Paul Gauguin, French Impressionist painter, died 1985.
◆ Ian Fleming, creator of 'Agent 007', born 1908.

9

◆ Sir James Barrie, creator of *Peter Pan*, born 1860.

10
◇ The Indian Mutiny began 1857.

11
● Sir John Herschel, British astronomer, died 1871.
◆ Irving Berlin, American song writer, born 1888.

12
◆ Edward Lear, author of *Book of Nonsense*, born 1812.
◆ Florence Nightingale, nursing pioneer, born 1820.

13
◆ Sir Arthur Sullivan, composer best known for his partnership with Sir William Gilbert in the writing of light operas, born 1842.

14
◆ Gabriel Fahrenheit, German physicist, who invented the mercury thermometer, born 1686.
◆ Thomas Gainsborough, English landscape and portrait painter, baptized 1727.
◇ The U.S. manned space station, *Skylab 2*, launched 1973.

15
◇ *Sputnik IV*, the first Russian space ship, launched 1960.

16
◆ John Sell Cotman, English water colourist, born 1782.
◇ The first film 'Oscars' were awarded, 1929.

17
● Sandro Botticelli, Italian artist, died 1510.
◆ Edward Jenner, discoverer of vaccination, born 1749.

18
◆ Walter Gropius, German-American architect and the founder of the 'Bauhaus', born 1883.

19
● Anne Boleyn, beheaded 1536.
● T. E. Lawrence ('Lawrence of Arabia') died following a road accident, 1935.

20
● Christopher Columbus, Genoan discoverer of the New World, died 1506.
● John Clare, English poet, died 1864.

21
◆ Elizabeth Fry, prison reformer, born 1780.
◇ Lady Jane Grey forced to marry Lord Guildford Dudley, 1553.
◇ Charles Lindbergh, American aviator, completed the first solo non-stop transatlantic flight, 1927.

22
◆ Sir Arthur Conan Doyle, creator of *Sherlock Holmes*, born 1859.
● Victor Hugo, French author of *Les Misérables*, died 1885.

Zoo opened to the

◆ ...l Linnaeus, founder of modern botany, born 1707.

● Henry Ibsen, Norwegian dramatist, died 1906.

24

◆ Queen Victoria born 1819.

● 'Duke' Ellington, American jazz composer, died 1974.

25

● Gustav Holst, English composer, died 1934.

26

● Samuel Pepys, diarist, died 1703.

27

◆ Georges Rouault, French painter, born 1871.

● Jawaharlal Nehru, first Prime Minister of India, died 1964.

28

● Anne Brontë, English novelist, died 1849.

● Duke of Windsor (King Edward VIII) died 1972.

29

● Sir William Gilbert, librettist of the 'Gilbert and Sullivan' light operas, died 1911.

◇ Sir Edmund Hilary and Sherpa Tensing were the first to reach the summit of Mount Everest, 1953.

30

● Saint Joan of Arc burnt at the stake at Rouen, France, 1431.

● Peter Paul Rubens, Flemish painter, died 1640.

31

● Tintoretto, Venetian painter, died 1594.

● Franz Joseph Haydn, Austrian composer, died 1809.

June

FLOWER: ROSE
BIRTHSTONE: PEARL

1

◆ Marilyn Monroe, American film star, born 1926.

2

◆ Sir Edward Elgar, English composer, born 1857.

◇ Queen Elizabeth II crowned at Westminster Abbey, 1953.

3

● William Harvey, discoverer of the circulation of the blood, died 1657.

4

◆ George III born 1738.

5

◆ Adam Smith, Scottish economist and author of *Wealth of Nations*, born 1723.

● Orlando Gibbons, English composer, died 1625.

6

◆ Robert Falcon Scott, Arctic explorer, born 1868.

◇ D-Day World War II, Allied forces invaded Nazi-held Western Europe, 1944.

7

● Robert Bruce, King of Scotland, died 1329.

◆ John Rennie, Scottish engineer, born 1761.

◆ Beau Brummel, leader of fashion in Bath, born 1778.

◆ Charles Rennie Mackintosh, pioneer of the Art Nouveau movement, born 1868.

8

◆ Sir John Millais, painter and a founder of the Pre-Raphaelite Brotherhood, born 1829.

◆ Frank Lloyd Wright, American architect, born 1869.

9

◆ George Stephenson, builder of the 'Rocket' locomotive, born 1781.

● Charles Dickens died 1870.

◆ Cole Porter, American composer, born 1892.

10

◆ Prince Philip, Duke of Edinburgh, born 1921.

11

◆ John Constable, English landscape painter, born 1776.

12

◆ Charles Kingsley, English novelist, born 1819.

◆ Anne Frank, Jewish author of the *Diary* telling of her life in hiding from the Nazis in 1942–44, born 1929.

13

● Alexander the Great died 32 BC.

◇ The first flying bomb (V-1) fell on London, 1944.

14

◇ The Battle of Naseby, 1645.

● John Logie Baird, Scottish television pioneer, died 1946.

15

◇ Magna Carta, the document on which much English law has been based, signed by King John, 1215.

◆ Edvard Grieg, Norweign composer, born 1843.

16

◇ Valentina Tereshkova, Soviet cosmonaut, became the first woman to travel in space, 1963.

◇ Soweto Uprising in South Africa when hundreds of children died, 1976.

17

◆ John Wesley, founder of Methodism, born 1703.

18

◇ Battle of Waterloo, 1815.

● William Cobbett, political pamphleteer and author of *Rural Rides*, died 1835.

19

◆ James VI of Scotland (James I of England), born 1566.

● Sir James Barrie, playwright and creator of *Peter Pan*, died 1937.

20

◇ Queen Victoria ascended the throne, 1837.

21

The Longest Day (except in Leap Year).

● Inigo Jones, the first of the great English architects, died 1652.

22

Longest Day in Leap Years.

◆ Sir Henry Rider Haggard, author of *King Solomon's Mine* and *She*, born 1856.

23

◆ Duke of Windsor (Edward VIII) born 1894.

24

Midsummer Day

◇ Battle of Bannockburn, 1314.

25

● General George Custer, American soldier, killed on the Little Bighorn River by Sioux Indians, 1876.

◆ 'George Orwell' (Eric Arthur Blair), author of *Nineteen Eighty-Four* and *Animal Farm*, born 1903.

26

● Gilbert White, naturalist of Selborne, died 1793.

27

◆ Helen Keller, American champion of the disabled, born 1880.

28

◆ Henry VIII born 1491.

29

◆ Peter Paul Rubens, Flemish painter, born 1577.

30

◆ John Gay, author of *The Beggar's Opera*, born 1685.

◆ Sir Stanley Spencer, English artist, born 1891.

July

FLOWER: LILY
BIRTHSTONE: RUBY

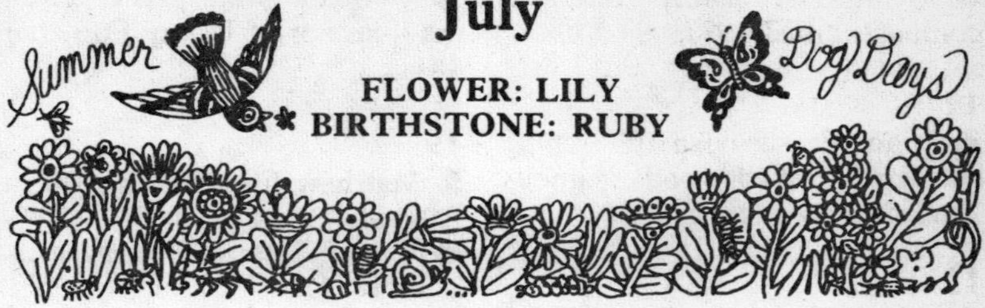

1
◆ Louis Blériot, the French aviator who made the first flight across the English Channel, born 1872.

2
◇ The Battle of Marston Moor, 1644.
◆ Jean-Jacques Rousseau, Swiss philosopher, born 1778.

3
◆ Robert Adam, Scottish architect, born 1728.

4
◆ Thomas Barnado, founder of the homes for destitute children, born 1845.
● Madam Curie, the Polish-born physicist and the discoverer, with her French husband Pierre, of radium, died 1934.

5
◆ ● Sir Stamford Raffles, colonial administrator, founder of the settlement on Singapore and co-founder of the London Zoo, born 1781, died 1826.

6
● Sir Thomas More beheaded in 1535 on the orders of Henry VIII whom More refused to recognise as the head of the English church.

7
◆ Marc Chagall, Russian-French artist, born 1887.
● Sir Arthur Conan-Doyle, creator of *Sherlock Holmes*, died 1930.

8
● Percy Bysshe Shelley, poet, died 1822.
◆ Sir Arthur Evans, British archaeologist who discovered Knossos in Crete, born 1851.

9
● Jan van Eyck, Flemish painter, died 1440.

10
◇ Lady Jane Grey proclaimed Queen of England, 1553.

11
◆ Robert Bruce, King of Scotland, born 1274.

● George Gershwin, American composer, died 1937.

12

◆ Julius Caesar born 100 BC.
◆ Josiah Wedgwood, famous English potter, born 1730.

13

◆ John Clare, poet, born 1793.
◇ First Live Aid Concert viewed by an estimated 2000 million TV viewers, 1985.

14

◆ Emmeline Pankhurst, champion of women's right to the vote, born 1858.

15

St. Swithin's Day.
◆ Inigo Jones, the first of the great English architects, born 1573.
◆ Rembrandt van Rijn, Dutch painter, born 1606.

16

◆ Sir Joshua Reynolds, English portrait painter, born 1723.

17

◆ Isaac Watts, English hymn-writer, born 1674.
● Billy Holliday, American jazz singer, died 1959.

18

◆ Gilbert White, naturalist, born 1720.
● Jane Austen, novelist, died 1817.
◆ William Makepeace Thackeray, author of *Vanity Fair*, born 1811.

19

● Matthew Flinders, explorer of Australia, died 1814.
◆ Edgar Degas, French artist, born 1834.

20

● Andrew Lang, collector of fairy tales, died 1912.

21

● Robert Burns, Scottish poet, died 1796.
◇ Neil Armstrong and Edwin 'Buzz' Aldrin were the first men to land on the moon in 1969.

22

◇ Battle of Falkirk, 1298.

23

◇ Battle of Shrewsbury, 1403.
◇ The ice cream cone was invented by Italo Marchioni at the World's Fair in St. Louis, Missouri, 1903.

24

◆ Alexandre Dumas, père, French writer, born 1802.

25

● Charles Macintosh, inventor of the waterproof garment, died 1843.
◇ Louis Blériot made the first flight across the Channel in 1909.

26

◆ George Bernard Shaw, Irish dramatist, born 1856.

27

● John Dalton, one of the greatest English chemists, died 1844.

28

◆ Beatrix Potter, creator of *Peter Rabbit*, born 1866.

29

◇ Spanish Armada defeated in 1588.

● William Wilberforce, philanthropist who struggled to abolish the slave trade, died 1833.

● Vincent van Gogh committed suicide, 1890.

30

◆ Henry Ford, pioneer of the motor car, born 1863.

◆ Emily Brontë, author of *Wuthering Heights*, born 1818.

31

● Franz Liszt, Hungarian composer, died 1886.

August

FLOWER: GLADIOLUS
BIRTHSTONE: ONYX

1

◆ Herman Melville, American author of *Moby Dick*, born 1819.

● Louis Blériot, French pioneer aviator, died 1936.

2

● Thomas Gainsborough, English painter, died 1788.

● Jacques Montgolfier, pioneer French balloonist, died 1799.

◆ Sir Arthur Bliss, English composer, born 1891.

3

● Grinling Gibbons, sculptor and woodcarver, died 1721.
◆ Rupert Brooke, English poet, born 1887.
◇ U.S. submarine, *Nautilus*, was the first ship to reach and pass under the North Pole, 1958.

4

◆ Percy Bysshe Shelley, English poet, born 1792.
● Hans Christian Andersen, Danish author of fairy stories, died 1874.
◆ Elizabeth, the Queen Mother, born 1900.

5

◆ Guy de Maupassant, French writer, born 1850.

6

● Anne Hathaway, wife of William Shakespeare, died 1628.
◆ Sir Alexander Fleming, discoverer of penicillin, born 1881.
◇ First atomic bomb dropped on Hiroshima, 1945.

7

◇ Henry Tudor (Henry VII) landed at Milford Haven, 1485.
◇ The first pictures of Earth were sent via U.S. satellite, the *Explorer VI*, 1959.

8

◇ Battle of Britain began 1940.

9

◆ Izaak Walton, author of *The Compleat Angler*, born 1593.
◆ Thomas Telford, Scottish engineer, born 1757.
● Frederick Marryat, writer of sea stories, died 1848.

10

◆ Laurence Binyon, English poet, born 1869.

11

◆ Joseph Nollekens, English sculptor, born 1737.
● Jackson Pollock, American abstract painter, died 1956.

12

◆ Thomas Bewick, wood engraver, born 1753.
● William Blake, painter and poet, died 1827.
● Ian Fleming, creator of *James Bond*, died 1964.

13

◇ Battle of Blenheim, 1704.
◆ John Logie Baird, television pioneer, born 1888.
● Florence Nightingale, nursing pioneer, died 1910.
● H. G. Wells, English writer, died 1946.

14

◆ John Galsworthy, author of the *Forsyth Saga*, born 1867.

● Richard Jefferies, naturalist and writer, died 1887.
◇ Japan surrendered, ending World War II, in 1945.

15
◆ T. E. Lawrence, 'Lawrence of Arabia', born 1888.
◆ Princess Anne born 1950.

16
● Elvis Presley, American 'pop' singer, died 1977.

17
● Ludwig Mies van der Rohe, German-born American architect, died 1969.

18
◆ Meriwether Lewis, American explorer, born 1774.

19
◆ John Flamsteed, first Astronomer Royal, born 1646.
● James Watt, inventor, pioneer of the steam engine and the nomenclator of a unit of power (a watt), died 1819.

20
● William Booth, founder of the Salvation Army, died 1912.
● Leon Trotsky, Russian revolutionary, assassinated in Mexico, 1940.

21
◆ Aubrey Beardsley, English illustrator, born 1872.
◆ Princess Margaret born 1930.
● Sir Jacob Epstein, English sculptor, died 1959.

22
◇ Battle of Bosworth, when Henry Tudor deposed Richard III as king in 1485.
◆ Claude Debussy, French composer, born 1862.

23
● Rudolph Valentino, the leading 'screen lover' of the 1920s, died 1926.

24
◆ William Wilberforce, slave trade abolitionist, born 1759.
◇ British troops captured Washington DC, 1814.

25
● Sir William Herschel, the astronomer who discovered the planet Uranus, died 1822.
● Michael Faraday, the scientist who made many important discoveries about electricity, died 1867.
◆ Leonard Bernstein, American composer, born 1918.

26
◇ Julius Caesar landed in Britain in 55BC.
◇ The Battle of Crecy, 1346.
◆ John Buchan, author of many adventure stories and Governor-General of Canada, born 1875.
● Ralph Vaughan Williams,

British composer, died 1958.
● Charles Lindbergh, American aviation pioneer, died 1974.

27
● Titian, one of the greatest Venetian painters, died 1576.
● Sir Rowland Hill, originator of penny postage in 1840, died 1879.
● Le Corbusier, French architect, died 1965.

28
◆ Count Leo Tolstoy, author of *War and Peace* and *Anna Karenina*, born 1828.

29
◇ 'The Ashes' instituted in cricket, 1882.
◇ The airship *Graf Zeppelin* completed circumnavigation of the world, 1929.

30
◆ Lord Rutherford, New Zealand-born physicist and one of the great pioneers of sub-atomic physics, born 1871.

31
◆ John Bunyan, author of *Pilgrim's Progress*, born 1688.

September

FLOWER: MORNING GLORY
BIRTHSTONE: SAPPHIRE

1
◆ Edgar Rice Burroughs, creator of *Tarzan*, born 1875.

2
◇ Great Fire of London began 1666 and lasted until September 6.
● Thomas Telford, one of the greatest Scottish civil engineers, died 1834.
● J. R. R. Tolkien, author of *The Hobbit* and *The Lord of the Rings*, died 1973.

3

● Oliver Cromwell died 1658.

◇ Britain and France declared war on Germany in 1939.

4

● Albert Schweitzer died at his mission hospital at Lambarene in 1965.

5

◆ Louis XIV, King of France, 'the Sun King', born 1643.

6

● Arthur Rackham, illustrator of fairy stories, died 1939.

7

◆ Elizabeth I, Queen of England, born 1533.

8

● Richard Straus, German composer, died 1949.

9

● William the Conqueror died 1087.

◇ Battle of Flodden Field, 1513.

◆ William Bligh, Captain of the *Bounty*, born 1754.

10

● Mungo Park, explorer of Africa, died when attacked by natives, 1806.

11

◆ D. H. Lawrence, English novelist, born 1885.

12

◇ The Egyptian obelisk known as 'Cleopatra's Needle' erected on the Thames embankment, 1878.

◇ The prehistoric Lascaux Cave paintings in France discovered by five boys, 1940.

13

● James Wolfe, English General, died at the Battle of Quebec at the point of victory, 1759.

14

◆ James Fenimore Cooper, American author of *The Last of the Mohicans* and other books about Red Indians, born 1851.

15

● Isambard Kingdom Brunel, one of the greatest English engineers and the builder of the Great Western Railway, died 1859.

16

● Daniel Fahrenheit, German physicist who first used quicksilver in thermometers and fixed freezing point at 32 degrees, died 1736.

◆ Sir Alexander Korda, Hungarian-born film producer, born 1893.

17

● William Henry Fox Talbot, pioneer of photography, died 1877.

18

◆ Dr. Samuel Johnson, writer,

critic, wit and the compiler of the first dictionary in the English language, born 1709.

19

● Thomas Barnardo, British founder of a society to rescue homeless boys, died 1905.

20

● Jacob Grimm, with his brother a collector of folk tales, died 1863.

◇ Ferdinand Magellan, the Portuguese explorer sailing under a Spanish flag, began the first voyage round the world, 1519.

21

◆ H. G. Wells, author of *The Time Machine* and many other books, born 1866.

22

◆ Michael Faraday, British scientist who is especially famous for his work on electricity, born 1791.

23

◆ Augustus Caesar, the first Roman Emperor, born 63 BC.

24

● Sir Howard Florey, Baron Florey of Adelaide, renowned for his work on penicillin therapy, died 1968.

25

◇ Battle of Stamford Bridge, 1066.

● Johann Straus, foremost composer of Viennese waltzes, died 1849.

26

◆ T. S. Eliot, American-born British poet whose work profoundly influenced poets of the 20th century and the author of *Old Possum's Book of Practical Cats* which has been adapted to the stage in a musical *Cats*, born 1888.

27

● Edgar Degas, French artist, died 1917.

28

● Louis Pasteur, French chemist famous for his work on rabies and anthrax diseases, died 1895.

29

Michaelmas Day (St. Michael and All Angels).

◆ Tintoretto, one of the greatest Venetian painters, born 1518.

◆ Lord Nelson born 1758.

30

◆ James Brindley, English canal builder, born 1772.

October

FLOWER: CALENDULA
BIRTHSTONE: OPAL

1

● Sir Edwin Landseer, Victorian animal painter and modeller of the lions at the foot of Nelson's Column, died 1873.

2

◆ Mahatma Gandhi, Indian nationalist leader, born 1869.

◆ Graham Greene, British novelist, born 1904.

3

● Saint Francis of Assissi died 1226.

4

● Rembrandt van Rijn, Dutch painter, died 1669.

● John Rennie, Scottish civil engineer, died 1821.

◇ First man-made satellite, *Sputnik I*, launched by the Russians, 1957.

5

● Jacques Offenbach, German composer of opera, died 1880.

6

● Alfred, Lord Tennyson, English poet, died 1893.

◇ First performances of a Promenade Concert, founded by Sir Henry Wood, 1895.

7

● Edgar Allan Poe, American author of macabre stories, died 1849.

◇ *Lunik III*, Russian spacecraft, took the first photographs of the far side of the Moon, 1959.

8

● Kathleen Ferrier, contralto singer, died 1953.

9

◆ Camille Saint-Saens, French composer of *A Carnival of Animals*, born 1835.

◆ John Lennon, one of the Beatles, born 1940.

10

◆ William Morris, Lord

Nuffield, the creator of the Morris Oxford in 1910 and the first British motor manufacturer to mass produce cheap cars, born 1877.

11

● Jean Cocteau, French poet, playwright and film director, died 1963.

12

◆ Ralph Vaughan Williams, British composer, born 1872.

● Elizabeth Fry, prison reformer, died 1845.

● Nurse Edith Cavell, executed by the Germans for helping refugees, 1915.

13

◆ Margaret Thatcher, first woman Prime Minister, born 1925.

14

◇ Battle of Hastings, 1066.

15

◆ P. G. Wodehouse, creator of *Jeeves* and *Bertie Wooster*, born 1881.

◆ Virgil, Roman Poet, born 70 BC.

16

◆ Robert Stephenson, builder of the Menai Straits Bridge, born 1803.

◆ Oscar Wilde, Irish playwright and wit, born 1854.

17

● Frédéric Chopin, Polish composer and pianist, died 1849.

18

● Charles Babbage, English inventor of a calculating machine, died 1871.

◆ Thomas Alva Edison, American inventor of the phonograph and a motion picture projector, died 1931.

19

● Jonathan Swift, author of *Gulliver's Travels*, died 1745.

20

◆ Sir Christopher Wren, astronomer and architect of many churches in London including St. Paul's Cathedral, born 1632.

21

◆ Hokusai, the famous Japanese painter, born 1760.

◇ Battle of Trafalgar, 1805.

● Admiral Lord Nelson died aboard his flagship H.M.S. *Victory*, 1805

22

◆ Franz Liszt, Hungarian composer, born 1881.

● Paul Cezanne, French artist, died 1906.

23

◆ W. G. Grace, a giant among cricketers, died 1915.

24

United Nations Day.

● Tycho Brahe, pioneer Danish astronomer, died 1601.

◆ Anton van Leeuwenhoek, Dutch naturalist and "Father of the Microscope," born 1632.

25

● Geoffrey Chaucer, author of *Canterbury Tales*, died 1400.

◆ Pablo Picasso, pioneer of Cubism and the leading figure in the history of 20th century art, born 1881.

26

● William Hogarth, English painter and engraver, died 1764.

27

◆ Sir William Smith, founder of the Boys' Brigade, born 1854.

28

● Alfred the Great died 901.

● James Cook, navigator and explorer, died 1728.

◆ Jonas Salk, American microbiologist who developed polio vaccine, born 1914.

29

● Sir Walter Raleigh, navigator and writer, executed 1618.

30

● Edmund Cartwright, English inventor of the power loom, died 1823.

◆ Ezra Pound, American poet, born 1885.

31

Halloween (All Hallows' Eve).

◆ John Evelyn, diarist, born 1620.

◆ John Keats, poet, born 1795.

● Harry Houdini, American escapologist, died 1926.

November

FLOWER: CHRYSANTHEMUM
BIRTHSTONE: TOPAZ

1

All Saints Day.

◆ Benvenuto Cellini, sculptor and goldsmith and one of the greatest craftsman of the Renaissance, born 1500.

2

◆ Daniel Boone, American pioneer and explorer, born 1734.

● George Bernard Shaw, Irish dramatist, died 1950.

3

● Henri Matisse, French artist, died 1954.

4

● Felix Mendelssohn, German composer, died 1847.

5

Guy Fawkes' Day.

● Mack Sennett, comedian and creator of 'The Keystone Kops', died 1960.

6

◆ James Naismith, Canadian-American inventor of basketball, born 1861.

◆ Richard Jefferies, naturalist and writer, born 1848.

7

◆ Marie Curie, co-discoverer with her husband of radium, born 1867.

8

◆ Edmond Halley, astronomer,

born 1656.
◆ John Milton, poet and author of *Paradise Lost* and *Paradise Regained*, born 1674.

9
◆ Sir Giles Gilbert Scott, architect of the Anglican Cathedral in Liverpool, born 1880.

10
◆ Jacob Epstein, English sculptor, born 1880.

11
Martinmas.
◇ Armistice Day: World War I.
● Ned Kelly, notorious Australian outlaw, hanged in Melbourne, 1880.

12
● Sir John Hawkins, British slave-trader and buccaneer knighted for his services against the Armada, died 1595.
● Baroness Orczy, author of *The Scarlet Pimpernel*, died 1947.

13
◆ Robert Louis Stevenson, poet and novelist and author of *A Child's Garden of Verses* and *Treasure Island*, born 1850.

14
◆ Roger Fulton, American inventor of the steamboat, born 1765.
◆ Claude Monet, French artist, born 1840.
◇ The B.C.C. began its first daily radio broadcasting service, 1922.
◆ Prince Charles born 1948.

15
◆ Sir William Herschel, who discovered the planet Uranus, born 1738.
◇ Sir Isaac Pitman first published his shorthand method 1837.

16
● Clark Gable, American film star, died 1960.

17
◆ Viscount Montgomery of Alamein born 1887.
● Auguste Rodin, French sculptor, died 1917.

18
◆ Louis Daguerre, French pioneer of photography, born 1789.

19
◇ Puerto Rico discovered by Christopher Columbus, 1493.
◇ President Lincoln delivered his Gettysburg address.

20
◆ Thomas Chatterton, 'the boy poet', born 1752.

21
● Henry Purcell, English composer, died 1695.

22
◆ 'George Eliot' (Mary Ann

Evans), author of *Adam Bede* and *Mill on the Floss*, born 1819.
◆ Benjamin Britten, English composer, born 1913.

23
● Richard Hakluyt, the geographer who introduced the use of the globe into English schools, died 1616.

24
◆ Grace Darling, heroine of the *Forfarshire* steamboat wreck in 1838, born 1815.

25
◆ Karl Benz, pioneer German motor manufacturer who produced one on the earliest petrol-driven vehicles in 1885, born 1844.

26
◇ The night of the Great Storm in 1703 when over 8,000 lives were lost in London and massive damage done in the South of England.

27
◇ Henry Winstanley, builder of the first Eddystone Lightstone, drowned when it was swept away in a gale in 1703.

28
◆ William Blake, poet and painter and author of *Songs of Innocence* and *Songs of Experience*, born 1757.

29
◆ Louisa M. Alcott, American writer of children's books and author of *Little Women*, born 1832.
◆ C. S. Lewis, author of *Out of the Silent Planet*, born 1898.

30
St. Andrew's Day.
◆ Andrea Palladio, one of the world's greatest architects, born 1508.
◆ 'Mark Twain' (Samuel Clemens), author of *Tom Sawyer* and *Huckleberry Finn*, born 1835.
◆ Sir Winston Churchill born 1874.

December

FLOWER: POINSETTIA
BIRTHSTONE: TURQUOISE

1
◇ The first women M.P., Lady Astor, took her seat in Parliament, 1919.

2
◆ Georges Seurat, the French artist and exponent of the 'pointillist' method of painting, born 1859.

3
◆ Joseph Conrad, Polish-English novelist and author of *Lord Jim*, born 1857.
● Robert Louis Stevenson, author of *Treasure Island*, *Kidnapped* and *Dr. Jekyll and Mr. Hyde*, died in Samoa, 1894.

4
● John Gay, author of *The Beggar's Opera*, died 1732.
● Benjamin Britten, English composer, died 1976.

5
◆ Walt Disney, American pioneer in animated film cartoons, born 1901.
● Claude Monet, French Impressionist painter, died 1926.

6
● Anthony Trollope, novelist, died 1882.

7
● William Bligh, captain of HMS *Bounty*, died 1817.

8
◆ Mary, Queen of Scots, born 1542.

9
◆ John Milton, poet, born 1608.

10
◆ Hans Memling, Flemish painter, born 1495.
◆ César Franck, French composer, born 1822.

11
◆ Charles Wesley, brother of John, the founder of Methodism, and author of over 5,000 hymns, born 1757.

12
◇ First transatlantic radio signal sent by Guglielmo Marconi, 1901.

13
◇ New Zealand discovered by the Dutch navigator, Abel Tasman, 1642.
● Samuel Johnson, the writer of the first dictionary in English, died 1784.

14
● George Washington, First President of the U.S.A., died 1799.

15
◆ Nero, Roman Emperor AD 54–68, born AD 37.
● Jan Vermeer, Dutch painter, died 1675.

16
◇ Boston Tea Party in U.S.A., 1733.
◆ Jane Austen, English novelist, born 1775.
◆ Noel Coward, playwright, born 1899.

17
◇ The Wright Brothers made their first flight at Kitty Hawk, N. Caroline, 1903.
◆ Ludwig van Beethoven baptized 1770.

18
● Antonio Stradivarius, famous violin maker, died 1737.

19
● Emily Brontë, author of *Wuthering Heights*, died 1848.
● J. M. W. Turner, English painter, died 1851.

20
◆ Sir Robert ('Bob') Menzies, Prime Minister of Australia 1939–41, 1949–66, born 1894.

21
Shortest day on average two years in every four.
● Giovanni Boccaccio, author of the *Decameron*, died 1375.
◆ Joseph Stalin, Russian leader, born 1879.

22
Shortest Day on an average of two years in every four.
● Beatrix Potter, creator of *Peter Rabbit*, died 1943.

23
◆ James Gibb, architect of St. Martin-in-the-Fields, London, born 1682.
◆ Sir Richard Arkwright, inventor, born 1732.

24
● Vasco de Gama, great Portuguese navigator, died 1524.
◆ George Crabbe, English poet, born 1754.

25
★ Christmas Day.
◆ Sir Isaac Newton, English

scientist and mathematician, born 1642.
● Sir Charles ('Charlie') Chaplin died 1977.

26
★ Boxing Day.
◆ Charles Babbage, English pioneer of computers, born 1792.

27
◆ Louis Pasteur, French discoverer of the existence of germs, born 1822.

28
◇ Chewing gum patented by American William Semple, 1869.

29
● Saint Thomas à Becket assassinated in Canterbury Cathedral, 1170.
◆ William Ewart Gladstone, four times Prime Minister, born 1809.

30
◆ Rudyard Kipling, author of the *Just So Stories*, born 1865.

31
● John Wycliffe, Protestant reformer, died 1384.
◆ Henri Matisse, French artist, born 1869.

Communications

This is a handy guide to some of the many ways in which people communicate with each other. Hobo signs, branding symbols, the meanings of colours; all these and more can be found on the following pages.

Important Events in Communication

B.C.

Before
3000 The Egyptians developed a picture language called hieroglyphics.

Before
1600 The Phoenicians invented an alphabet.

300 Numerals were invented in India.

A.D.

1755 Samuel Johnson published a dictionary of the English language, the first English dictionary.

1828 Noah Webster published the first American dictionary.

1844 Samuel Morse sent the first telegraph message.

1876 The telephone was invented by American, Alexander Graham Bell.

1895 In Italy, Guglielmo Marconi invented the wireless telegraph.

1927 Movies with sound first appeared in American theatres.

1934 First official BBC television service.

1955 First British commercial TV broadcast on September 22 at 7.15 pm.

1957 The first artificial earth satellite sent back information from space.

1959 STD first introduced in Great Britain by the Post Office.

1962 Television programmes were relayed between the U.S. and Europe via the satellite, *Telstar I*.

1965 The U.S. launched *Early Bird*, the first commercial communications satellite.

1967 First BBC colour transmission on 625 lines on July 1.

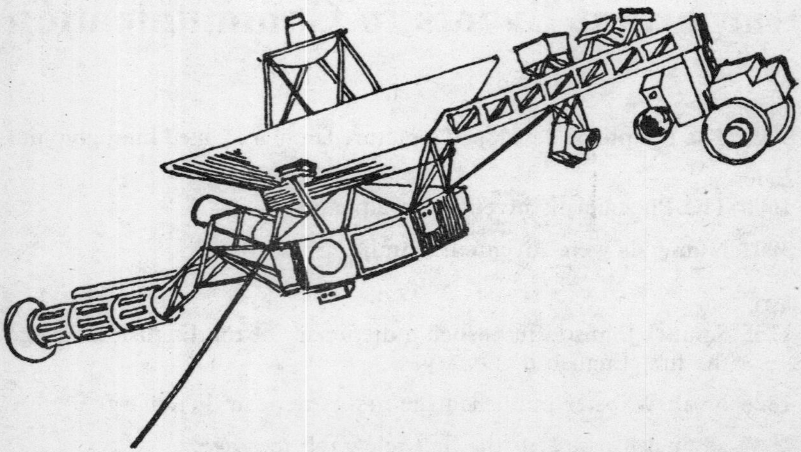

Signs, Symbols, Language

SIGNS

Semaphore

Alphabet of Hand Flags
Flags are used to send messages to people who are within seeing range but not within hearing range. This form of communication is commonly used by sailors, lifeguards, and boy scouts.

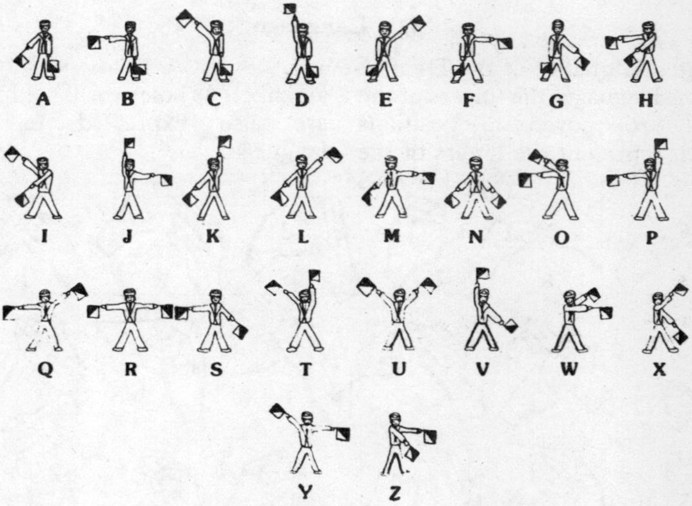

Morse Code

Alphabet of Telecommunication
Using this code of dots and dashes, messages are telegraphed over long distances. Each dot is a short sound; each dash is a long sound. Combinations of dots and dashes form the letters of the alphabet.

A ·–	**J** ·–––	**R** ·–·
B –···	**K** –·–	**S** ···
C –·–·	**L** ·–··	**T** –
D –··	**M** ––	**U** ··–
E ·	**N** –·	**V** ···–
F ··–·	**O** –––	**W** ·––
G ––·	**P** ·––·	**X** –··–
H ····	**Q** ––·–	**Y** –·––
I ··		**Z** ––··

Braille

Alphabet of the Blind

People who are blind have a special system for reading. A series of raised dots on paper symbolize letters. They are combined to form words. Finger-tips are used to feel this language.

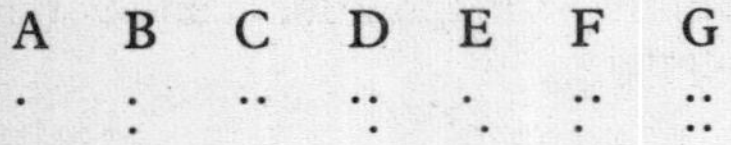

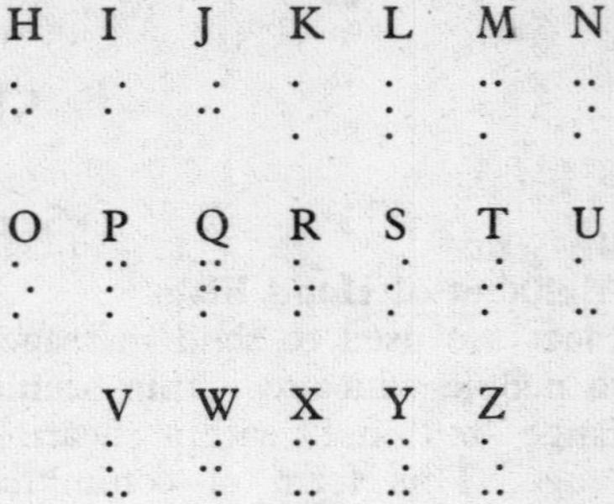

Sign Language

Manual Alphabet of the Deaf

In this language, the fingers of the hand are moved to positions which represent the letters of the alphabet. Whole words and ideas are also expressed in sign language.

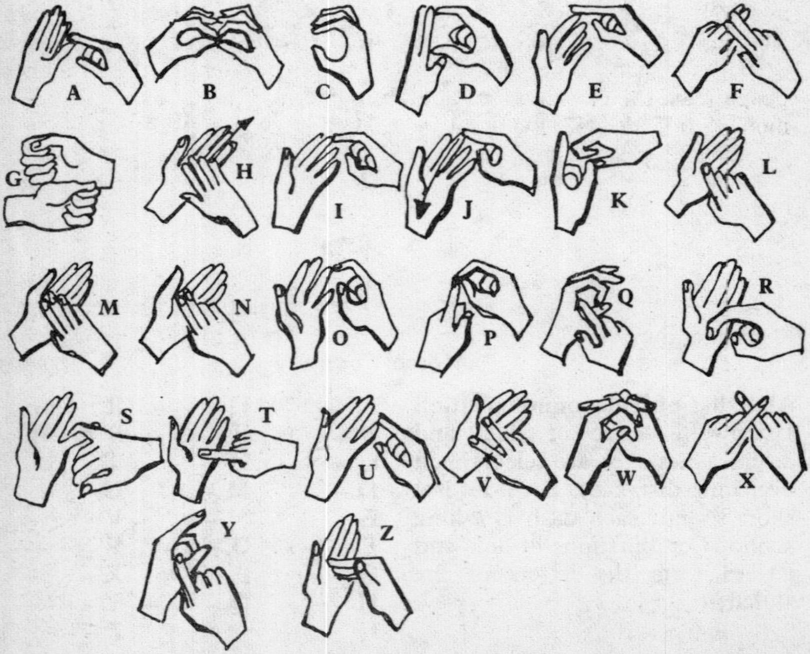

BASIC SYMBOLS

1. And	&	8. Equals	=	17. Multipled by	×
2. Asterisk	*	9. Feet	′	18. Paragraph	¶
3. At, each	©	10. Female	♀	19. Parallel	‖
4. Cents	c	11. In care of	c/o	20. Prescription	℞
5. Degree	°	12. Inches	″	21. Proportion	::
6. Divide	÷	13. Infinity	∞	22. Plus/Positive	+
7. Dollar	$	14. Is greater than	>	23. Ratio of	:
		15. Is less than	<		
		16. Male	♂		

Hobo Picture Language

American tramps, or 'hobos', invented their own secret language to communicate with each other. Hobos are homeless people who travel around without money or means, looking for shelter and food as they go.

1. Good road to follow 
2. Dangerous neighbourhood 
3. Nothing good here 
4. Good place for a handout 
5. Food here, if you work 

Branding Signs

Ranch owners mark their herds with symbols to show ownership. They created a special language of symbols to identify their ranches.

Here are some examples.

An upside down brand means 'crazy' as in Crazy Heart. 

Wings on a brand means 'flying' as in Flying V. 

A curved line under a brand means 'rocking' as in Rocking R. 

A curved line over a brand means 'swinging' as in Swinging Star. 

Witches Signs

These signs of witchcraft have been used for centuries to ward off trouble or to attract good luck. In the 17th century, the Amish people brought these symbols from Germany to the Pennsylvania farm land where they settled. Today, these symbols are used as decorations rather than for protection.

Fertility

Sunshine

Rain

Justice

Good Luck

Wisdom

Against Demons

Against Lightning

Roman Numerals

The ancient Romans used a system of letters for counting. Their numbering system is commonly used today on the faces of clocks and to mark chapters in books. The basic Roman numerals and their number values are listed below.

I—1	**VI—6**	**L—50**
II—2	**VII—7**	**C—100**
III—3	**VIII—8**	**D—500**
IV—4	**IX—9**	**M—1,000**
V—5	**X—10**	

Symbols of Religions

The major religions of the world have symbols to identify them. Here are seven religions and their most common symbols.

Buddhism

Christianity

Confucianism

Hinduism

Islam

Judaism

Taoism

Colour Symbols

Colours communicate meaning. For example, a red traffic light means STOP. Colours also express feelings and are often associated with special events.

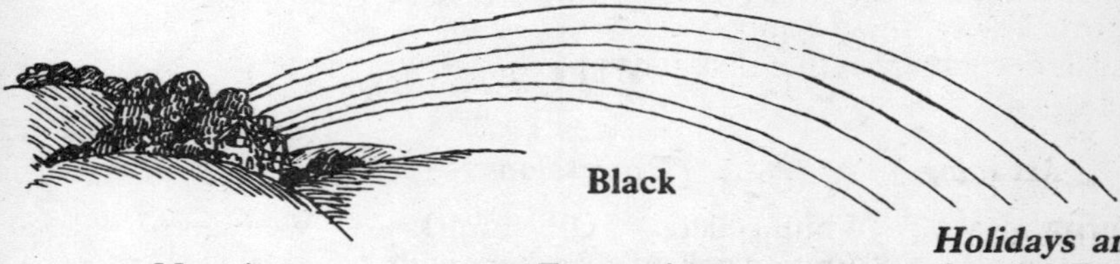

Meaning	*Expressions*		*Holidays and Special Days*
	Black		
Sophistication, night, death	'Blackball'	To vote against	Halloween
	'Blacklist'	List of people held in disfavour	
	'Blackmail'	Extortion	
	'Black Sheep'	A disgrace; an outcast	
	'In the Black'	Making money	
	Blue		
Sky, truth, discouragement	'Feeling blue'	Sadness	
	'Blue blood'	Aristocracy, upper class	
	'True blue'	Loyal	
	'Once in a blue moon'	Infrequently	
	Green		
Envy, nature, prosperity, youth	'Green thumb'	Good plant grower	Christmas
	'Greenbacks'	Paper money	St. Patrick's Day
	'Greenhorn'	Inexperienced person	

Red

Life, warmth, fire	'In the red'	Losing money	Christmas
	'Paint the town red'	A wild time	St. Valentine's
	'Red carpet'	Royal treatment	
	'Red faced'	Embarrassed	

White

Meaning	*Expressions*		*Holidays and Special Days*
Purity, peace	'White collar'	Office work	Weddings
	'White elephant'	An item with little or no value	
	'White flag'	Surrender	
	'White lie'	Harmless untruth	

Yellow

Cowardice, wisdom	'Yellow bellied'	Cowardly	Easter
	'Yellow dog'	Scoundrel	
	'Yellow journalism'	Sensationalism	
	'Yellow streak'	Tendency toward cowardice	

Languages

The number of languages spoken in the world is estimated to be in the thousands. This is a list of the major languages spoken by the greatest number of people. They are ranked in order of usage.

Name of Language	*Major locations where spoken*
Chinese (Mandarin)	China
English (has the most words—790,000—in its language.)	U.S., U.K., Canada, Ireland, Australia, New Zealand

Hindi	India
Spanish	Spain, South America
Russian	Russia
Arabic	Middle East, North Africa
Bengali	Bangladesh, India
Portuguese	Portugal, Brazil, parts of Africa and Asia
German	Germany, Austria, Switzerland,
Japanese	Japan
French	France, Belgium, Switzerland, Canada

HOW TO SAY HELLO, GOODBYE, AND THANK YOU IN 20 LANGUAGES

Language	*Hello*	*Goodbye*	*Thank You*
Chinese	Nihow	Tzay-jiann	Shieh-shieh
Czech	Dobry den	Sbohem	Dekuji
Dutch	Goëd dag	Dag	Dank
Esperanto (world language)	Saluton	Adiau	Dunkon
French	Bon jour	Au revoir	Merci
German	Guten Tag	Auf Wiedersehen	Danke

Greek	Yaisou	Andio	Bfeharisto
Hebrew	Shalom	Shalom	Todah
Italian	Bon giorno	Addio	Grazie
Japanese	Ohio	Sayonara	Kansha suru
Norwegian	God Morgen	Farvel	Takk
Polish	Dubry den	Do widzenia	Dziekuje
Portuguese	Bom dia	Adeus	Obrigado
Rumanian	Buna	Adio	Multumiri
Russian	Zdrastvoukee	Do zuidaniya	Spasibo
Spanish	Buenos dias	Adios	Gracias
Swahili	Jambo	Kwaheri	Asante
Swedish	God dag	Adjo	Tack
Turkish	Alo	Allah ismarladik	Tchawk
Yiddish	Sholem-alé ykhem	Seid ge zund	Dank

FUN WITH WORDS

Acronyms are words formed by the first letters of a series of words. Some commonly-used acronyms are:

EFTA—European Free Trading Association

NATO—North Atlantic Treaty Organisation

OPEC—Organisation of Petroleum Exporting Countries

RADA—Royal Academy of Dramatic Art

SALT—Strategic Arms Limitation Talks

UNO—United Nations Organisation

Palindromes

Palindromes are words or groups of words which can be spelled the same backwards or forwards. The following are two examples of palindromes:

'Able was I ere I saw Elba'
Jokingly attributed to Napoleon

'Madam, I'm Adam'
Adam's reputed greeting to Eve in the Garden of Eden!

Anagrams

Anagrams are words or phrases that can be scrambled to make other words or phrases. Some examples are:

Angered—enraged, derange, grenade, grandee
Lustre—result, rustle, rulest, Ulster

Animal anagrams:	low (owl)	acts (cats)
	bare (bear)	sales (seals)

Semordnilaps

Semordnilaps are Lewis Carroll's version of palindromes. These are words that spell other words when reversed.

Evil—live	deliver—reviled
pin—nip	not—ton

Computers and Robots

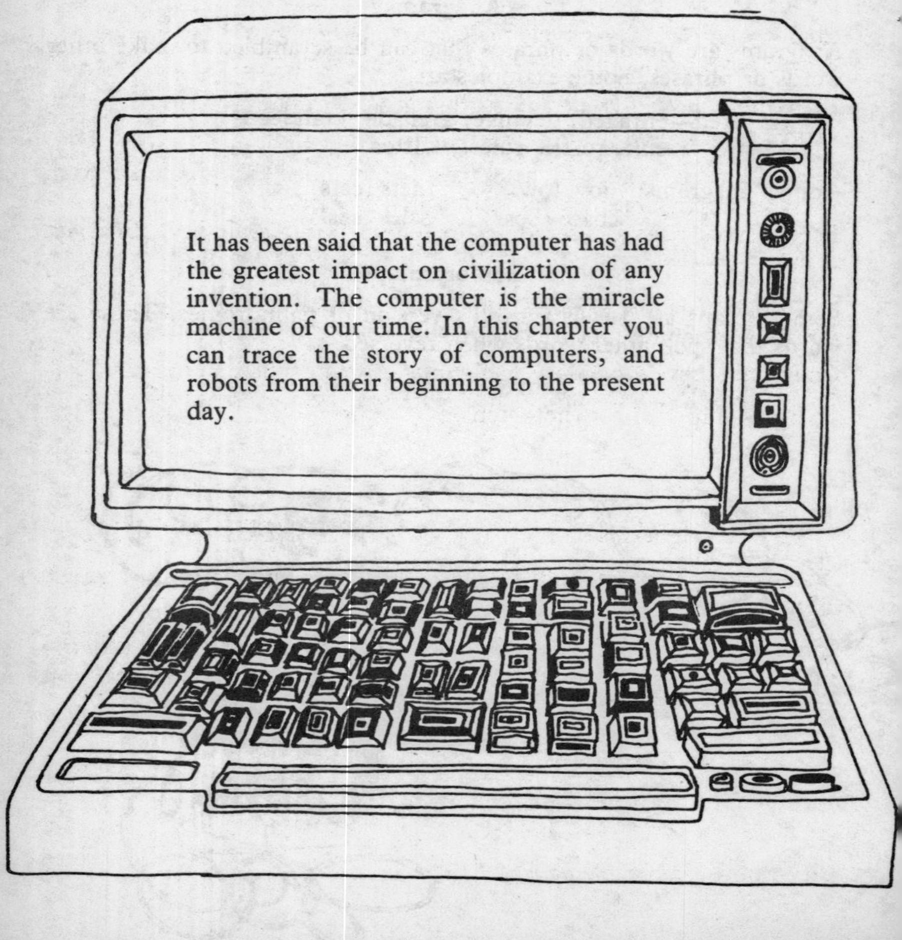

It has been said that the computer has had the greatest impact on civilization of any invention. The computer is the miracle machine of our time. In this chapter you can trace the story of computers, and robots from their beginning to the present day.

Computers

COMPUTERS AND PEOPLE

Computers must be told what to do. They cannot think independently of their programming.
People can think, thus making the computer's programming work.

Computers can 'see,' 'hear,' and 'feel' by the use of electromagnets, photoelectric cells, crystals, and copper wire brushes.
People use eyes, ears, and fingers to see, hear, and feel.

Computers use electricity as their source of energy.
People have brains that use blood glucose for energy.

Computers never forget unless programmed to do so.
People forget without meaning to.

Computers are sensitive machines. They must be protected from extreme temperatures, moisture, dirt, and dust.
People have bodies that adjust to temperature, humidity, dirt, and dust.

Computers have no intelligence of their own.
People have an average intelligence of 100 on the I.Q. scale.

Computers have a memory that can work faster than a person's.
People have a memory that can hold more than a computer's.

A BASIC GLOSSARY OF COMPUTER WORDS

Add Time—The amount of time it takes a computer to do a single addition operation.

Binary Numbers—The numbers 0 and 1 are the only two (binary) numbers used by a computer. Letters and numbers are combinations of these binary numbers. For example:

A—1000001	**0**—0000
B—1000010	**1**—0001
C—1000011	**2**—0010
D—1000100	**3**—0011

Bit—Short for binary digit

Bug—A mistake in a computer program. It got its name when a real bug—a moth—got stuck in a Harvard University computer and the computer stopped working.

Byte—A group of eight binary digits used to represent one unit of data in the computer memory. The size of the computer is measured in bytes.

Chip—A tiny piece of silicon (sand) which is covered with thousands of passageways (some as long as 24 miles) through which electronic messages travel.

Computer—A machine that obeys a list of commands stored in its memory.

CPU (Central Processing Unit)—The control centre of the computer which organizes all the other parts inside the computer.

Data—The information the computer needs to do its work.

Disc Drive—This works much like a record turntable. If the program is on a disc, a disc drive is needed to run it.

Flowchart—A chart which shows the steps needed in the program.

Hardware—All the computer equipment including the computer itself, input and output equipment, disc and tape equipment.

Input—The information that goes into the computer. Also, the process of putting information into the computer.

K—This is an abbreviation for 1,000. A 10K computer stores 10,000 bytes of computer memory.

Keyboard—A row of buttons used to put information into the computer.

Memory—The chips in the computer where information and instructions are in binary code.

Modem—A device which allows computers to 'talk' to one another over the telephone. It turns computer signals into phone vibrations.

Microprocessor—A small silicon chip which does the same job as the CPU and main memory of a computer.

Output—The information the computer puts out after processing it.

Program—A list of orders fed into or stored within the computer.

RAM (Random Access Memory)—The part of a computer's memory where information is temporarily stored.

ROM (Read Only Memory)—The part of a computer's memory which holds a permanent store of instructions which cannot be erased by the user.

Software—Computer programs.

VDU (Visual Display Unit)—A screen similar to a TV screen which is used to display computer information.

A GUIDE TO COMPUTER LANGUAGES

Special languages are used to program computers. There are over 1,000 languages in use today. Ten of the most common ones are listed here.

ALGOL is short for Algorithmic Language and is used for scientific purposes.

BASIC stands for Beginners All Purpose Symbolic Instruction Code. It is a general purpose language used by students and non-specialists.

COBOL means Common Business Oriented Language. It is the most commonly used language of professionals.

FORTRAN stands for Formula Translator and is used for scientific and business purposes.

JOVIAL is an acronym for Jules Own Version of the International Algebraic Language. It was invented by Jules Schwartz and is used by the military.

LISP stands for List Processor. It was the first language developed for working with artificial intelligence.

LOGO is a Greek word which literally means 'word.' It is used primarily by young children.

PASCAL is named after the mathematician Blaise Pascal. It is used for systems development.

PILOT stands for Programming Inquiry Learning or Teaching. It uses short, simple commands; a good language for beginners.

SMALL TALK is used for communicating with personal computers in a visual way.

COMPUTER FIRSTS

1852 The world's first programmer was Lady Augusta Ada Lovelace of England. She worked with Charles Babbage who invented the analytical machine, a forerunner of modern computers. She is credited with telling a machine what to do by using punch cards to programme algebraic patterns. The U.S. Department of Defense uses a programming language named ADA in her honour.

1946 The first electronic computer was made at the University of Pennsylvania. The 30-ton machine stood two storeys high and was named ENIAC (Electronic Numerical Integrator and Calculator).

1951 The first computer animated movies were made at the Massachusetts Institute of Technology.

1968 The first computer to star in a movie was H.A.L. who was featured in the movie *2001*: *A Space Odyssey*.

1970 The first all-computer art exhibit took place at the Jewish Museum in New York City. The show featured computer software.

1976 The first broadway show to use computers was *A Chorus Line*. The computers were used for lighting.

1981 George Guillamo of Valenciennes, France, was the first restaurant owner to use computers to take orders from his customers. Each dining table was equipped with a computer. The menu of the day appeared on the screen and customers typed in their selection.

1982 The first BBC televised computer course was called 'The Computer Programme' and was first transmitted on BBC2 from January.

1984 The first commercial record made entirely by computer was called 'Classical Mosquito.' It was conceived and directed by Robb Murray, a composer from Chicago, Illinois.

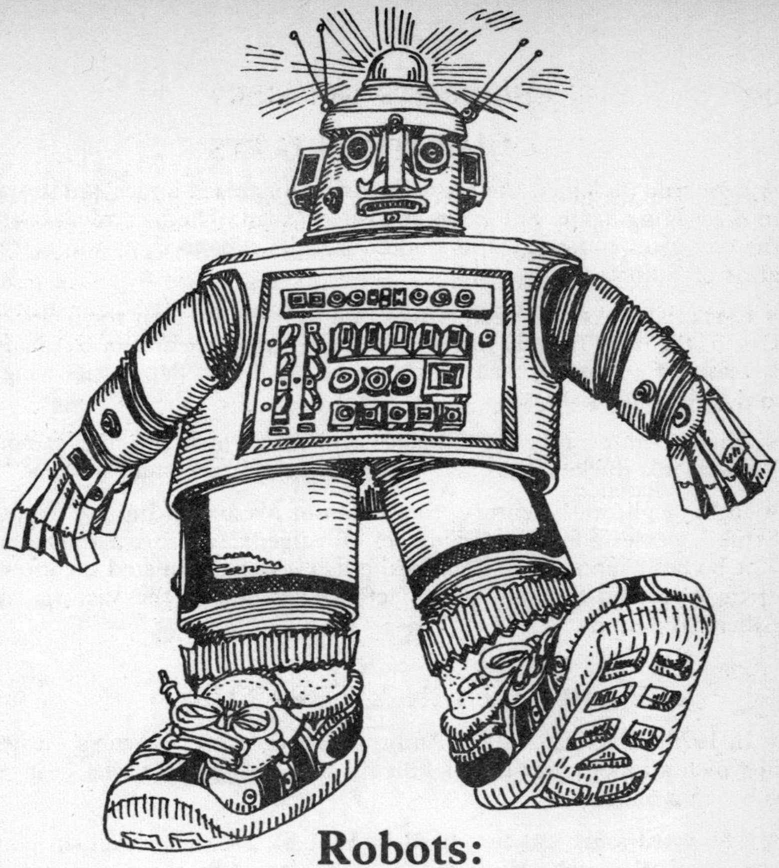

Robots:

MACHINES THAT LOOK AND PERFORM LIKE LIVING CREATURES

ROBOTS IN MYTH AND LEGEND

• King Minos of ancient Crete used a brass robot named Talos to patrol and protect his island. Talos met his fate when an enemy of Minos drained Talos' power by pulling a plug from his foot.

• Daedalus, according to the Greek myths, built strange statutes that moved by themselves. The Greek philosopher Plato described Daedalus' figures as so life-like that they had to be restrained to prevent them from running away.

• In Homer's 'Iliad,' two robots of pure gold were messengers for Hephaestus, the God of fire.

EARLY ROBOTS

• Leonardo da Vinci, the artist and inventor, made a mechanical lion to greet King Louis XII when he visited Milan. The lion advanced to the city gates and opened its middle with its claw to show the coat of arms of France.

• Clockmakers of the Middle Ages built robots into their town clocks. One of the most famous was in the Strasbourg Cathedral in Germany. It featured a crowing bird which opened its beak, flapped its wings, and spread its feathers.

• Eighteenth-century toys made in France included the famous Vaucanson's duck. It was able to eat, drink, 'quack,' and walk.

• In the eighteenth century, the Sultan of Mysore in India, "Tippoo Sahib", possessed a wooden model of a tiger devouring a European. The bodies concealed a mechanical organ which stimulated the growls of the tiger and the cries of its victim. It is now in the Victoria and Albert Museum.

ROBOTS IN LITERATURE

• In 1920, American author Ambrose Bierce wrote 'Movon's Master' in which a robot chess player kills his human opponent who beat the robot in a match.

• The word *robot* was first used in 1921 by a Czechoslovakian playwright, Karl Capek. His play, 'R.U.R.', told the story of a greedy factory owner who made robots to replace human workers. The robots eventually turned on their human masters and destroyed them. In Czech, the word *robota* means worker.

• Isaac Asimov has written many short stories about robots. They have been collected into two volumes: *I Robot* (1950), and *The Best of Robots* (1964). These stories describe the importance of robots in industry.

ROBOTS IN FILMS

The Golem, 1920. This was the first film to feature a robot.

Metropolis, 1926. A female robot was first featured in this film.

The Day the Earth Stood Still, 1952. This film shows a spaceship which lands in Washington, D.C., with a robot carrying a vital message for humankind.

Forbidden Planet, 1956. A science fiction film classic introducing Robbie the Robot.

Star Wars, 1977. This science fiction film introduced R2D2 and C-3PO.

The Empire Strikes Back, a 1980 sequel to the successful *Star Wars*.

FAMOUS WORLD'S FAIR ROBOTS

- The Chicago World's Fair in 1934 featured a robot built by Roland Scaffer. Among other things, his robot could walk, hammer nails, saw tree trunks, and clean windows.
- The largest robot shown at a world's fair was built for Expo '70 in Osaka, Japan. It was twenty-four feet tall.

TYPES OF ROBOTS

Automaton—Any machine that works on its own. For example, a cuckoo clock.

Android—A machine built to look or act like a human. For example, Sim One, an artificial hospital patient.

Cyborg—Part human, part robot. For example, Steve Austin in the TV show, 'The Six Million Dollar Man.'

Droid—Robots completely devoted to their human masters. For example, R2D2 and C-3PO from *Star Wars*.

Probots—Personal robots for home use. For example, Robbie the Robot in the movie, *Forbidden Planet*.

Robotrix—A female robot, such as The False Maria in the Fritz Lang movie, *Metropolis*.

ISAAC ASIMOV'S RULES FOR ROBOTS

1. A robot may not injure a human being.
2. A robot must obey human commands except when the orders conflict with rule No. 1.
3. A robot must protect itself unless such protection conflicts with rule No. 1 and rule No. 2.

Food

Here you will find stories of how food was created and how other foods got their names, as well as advice on the best foods to eat to keep you healthy.

Facts About Food

How Five Foods Were Created

1. The first doughnuts with holes were made by a 15-year-old, Hanson Crockett. He was a baker's apprentice working in Camden, Maine, in 1847. One day he noticed a rawness in the middle of his fried cakes. He cut out the soggy centres and made the first ring doughnuts. They became very popular and were made by hand until the first doughnut cutter was invented in 1872.
2. The ice cream sundae was first made in E. C. Berner's ice cream parlour in Two River, Wisconsin, around 1890. One of Berner's customers suggested that he pour chocolate syrup over a scoop of ice cream in a dish. This ice cream treat was a hit but was originally sold only on Sundays, hence the name.
3. Peanut Butter was the creation of a St. Louis doctor who was trying to improve the diets of his patients. He spread mashed peanuts on bread and suggested that his patients eat this nutritional, high protein, inexpensive food.
4. One cold night in 1905, Frank Epperson of San Francisco, California, accidentally left a mixing stick in a glass of lemonade on his window sill. The following morning, the lemonade was found frozen into the first known 'ice lollipop.'
5. The first potato chips were made in a fit of frustration. George Crumb was a chef working at the Moon Lake Lodge in Saratoga Springs, New York. One evening in 1835, a customer kept sending french fries back to the kitchen complaining they were too thick and too soft. Finally, the chef took a potato, sliced it wafer thin, fried it, and personally served the first potato chips to the satisfied customer.

Five Facts About Hamburgers

1. The first 'hamburgers' were eaten by the Tartars, a Mongol people. Their version of the 'hamburger' was raw, shredded goat, camel, or horsemeat made into a patty.
2. The first major hamburger chain in the U.S.A. was White Castle, which was established in 1921. The White Castle hamburger was shaped into a thin 2½-inch square and sold for 5 cents.

3. An American-style hamburger sold in countries such as France, Italy, and Japan may contain a high proportion of pork and possibly rabbit and horsemeat plus fat and cereal fillers. This is because beef is not as readily available in those countries as it is in the U.S.

4. A degree of 'Bachelor of Hamburgerology' is awarded to all graduates of McDonald's Hamburger University. All managers and owners of McDonald's restaurants must earn this degree.

5. Raw chopped meat patties were first seasoned and cooked in Hamburg, Germany. The Germans called them 'Deutsche' or beefsteak. When introduced to America, they were first known as Hamburg steaks and later called Hamburgers.

How Five Foods Got Their Names

1. The cracker was named by Josiah Bent of Milton, Massachusetts. It was in the early 1890s when he baked an extra crispy batch of biscuits. They crackled when eaten so he called them crackers.

2. The 18th century was the great age of gambling in Britain. The 4th Earl of Sandwich was so determined not to leave the gaming tables, even for a meal, he ordered 'slices of beef placed between pieces of bread'. Thus was the sandwich invented.

3. French fries are not named after the country of France. 'Frenched' means to cut into narrow strips, before frying. These long, thin potatoes are named for the cooking term.

4. The hot dog got its name from Chicago newspaper cartoonist Tad Dorgan. One day in 1906, Dorgan was attending a baseball game

in New York's Polo Grounds. He drew a sketch of frankfurters making them look like dachshunds on buns. Beneath the cartoon he wrote, 'Hot Dogs.'

5. Ketchup originated in China. The Chinese made a spicy sauce of fish broth and mushrooms which they called ke-tsiap. Sailors brought the recipe for this sauce to England where tomatoes were added. The name for them became *kechup*.

Facts about the food we eat

We need food to create strong healthy bodies, but we must eat the right food.

Heart disease, some forms of cancer, and many other ailments are caused by the wrong diet. Fat, such as butter and whole milk; food cooked in fat, such as chips and sausages; and 'fast' food such as beefburgers and hot dogs, are all bad for health if eaten too often.

We eat too much sugar—in tea and soft drinks, in chocolate and sweets generally, and in biscuits and cakes. Sugar causes tooth decay, overweight and spots.

We don't eat enough food with a high fibre content such as porridge, bran and wholemeal bread, vegetables, beans (pulses) and fresh fruit.

Our diets should include fish, lean meat, vegetables and fruit.

We should reduce the amount of salt we eat by avoiding adding salt to our food and cutting down on salty foods, such as peanuts and potato crisps.

We should drink skimmed or semi-skimmed pasteurised milk from which excessive fat has been removed.

Facts About Soft Drinks

1. Carbonated water, the basis for modern soft drinks, was first made by an Englishman, Joseph Priestley, in 1772. By adding carbonic gas to water, Priestley was able to duplicate nature's bubbling water.
2. The first sweetened carbonated drink was ginger ale. It was created in Ireland by Dr. Cantrall in 1850.
3. Coca cola syrup was first made in 1886 by pharmacist John Pemberton of Atlanta, Georgia. He created the syrup as a cure for headaches and hangovers. His employee, William Venable, who worked at the pharmacy soda fountain, added carbonated water to

the syrup and made the first coca cola soft drink. There are fifteen ingredients in Coca Cola. Fourteen of them are well known, but one which is called 7x is still a well-guarded secret.

Five Kinds of Bottled Water

1. Distilled water is vaporized and condensed to remove all minerals.
2. Soda water, also known as club soda in the U.S.A., is tap water which has been charged with carbon dioxide gas.
3. Natural spring water is bottled at a natural spring or other pure water source.
4. Natural mineral water is bottled at a protected spring. It is prized for its particular mineral content and is often naturally bubbly.
5. Purified water is drawn from wells or taps. It is cleansed of all minerals; specific minerals are then replaced.

Five Startling Facts About Food

1. People in Britain suffer from more heart disease than in many other countries.
2. One in three of us is overweight.
3. 95 out of every 100 have tooth decay.
4. The average person in Britain consumes 38 kilos of sugar a year.
5. A Mars bar contains 9 teaspoons of sugar.

Five Food Terms

1. **Enriched foods** have nutrients restored which have been lost in processing.
2. **Fortified foods** have vitamins and minerals added to them to make them more nutritious.
3. **Junk foods** are foods which have sugar or fat as the main ingredient. For example, candy is mainly sugar, and potato chips are mostly fat.
4. **Kosher foods** are certain foods which are prepared under the supervision of a rabbi, according to Jewish dietary laws.
5. **Natural foods** are unprocessed foods which have no preservatives, or artificial colours or flavours.

Pancakes Round the World

Blinis—Russia
Blinzes—Jew
Crêpe—France
Drop scones—Scotland
Eierkuckas—Alsatia
Hoe cakes—U.S.A.

Myths About Foods

1. Eating beetroots will make one's blood redder.
2. Bread and potatoes are fattening foods.
3. Brown eggs are more nutritious than white eggs.
4. Honey is less fattening than sugar.

Traditional Foods for Special Days

Shrove Tuesday—Pancakes
Good Friday—Hot Cross Buns
Easter—Simnel Cakes
November 5—Parkin
Christmas—Turkey, Christmas Pudding

Foods that were brought back from the New World

Maize
Coffee
Pineapple
Pumpkin

Potato
Turkey
Peanut

Five Facts About Chocolate

1. The first people to drink chocolate were the Mayans and Aztecs, natives of Central America.
2. Chocolate, in the form of cacao beans, was once used as money in South America.
3. It is said that Montezuma, the Aztec king, drank 50 cups of chocolate a day.
4. Hernando Cortez, the Spanish explorer, first brought chocolate from Mexico to Europe in the early 1500s.
5. Casanova, the famous 18th-century Italian lover, drank chocolate as a love potion.

Meats

Meat is often the main course at a major meal. How the meat is prepared and how it tastes, varies according to the part of the animal used. The following lists are of the major animals used for food and the variety of meats people consume.

VEAL

This meat comes from a calf.

Part	*Use*
Shoulder	Roast
Ribs	Chops, cutlets
Loin	Chops, cutlets
Leg	Roast, escalops
Breast	Roast, stew
Leg/shin	Stewing meat

PORK

This meat comes from a pig.

Part	*Use*
Hand or shoulder	Roast Shoulder chops
Fat back	Lard, salt pork, tenderloin
Loin	Chops, roast
Leg	Roasts, smoked ham
Side	Bacon
Spareribs	Pork ribs

LAMB

This meat comes from sheep less than a year old.

Part	*Use*
Shoulder	Roast
Back	Rib chops, crown roast
Loin	Saddle roast
Leg	Roast
Breast	Roast (stuffed and rolled)

MISCELLANEOUS

Brains—Offal of beef, lamb, pork, and veal.
Heart—Offal of beef, lamb, poultry, and veal.
Kidney—Offal of beef, lamb, pork, and veal.
Liver—Offal of beef, lamb, poultry, and veal.
Sweetbreads—The thymus glands of young animals, usually calves.
Tongue—From beef, lamb, pork, and veal.
Tripe—Lining of the inner stomach of a cow.

BEEF

This meat comes from a bullock.

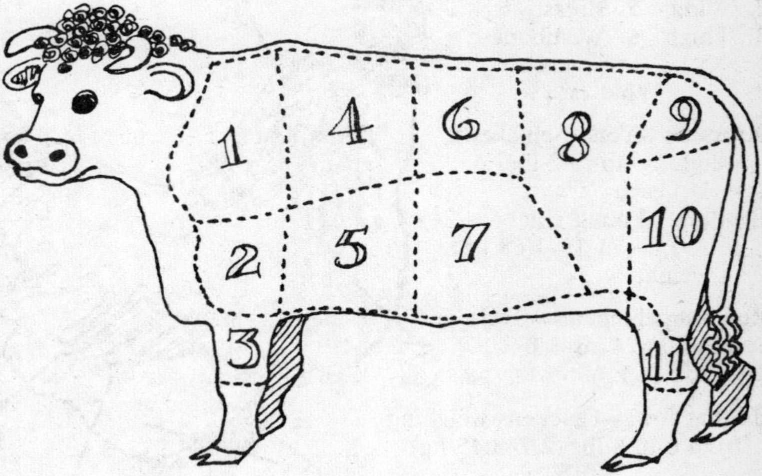

Cuts of Beef

1. Shoulder and neck
2. Brisket
3. Shin
4. Ribs
5. Flat ribs
6. Wing rib
7. Skirt
8. Sirloin
9. Rump
10. Silverside
11. Leg

Traditional British Regional Foods

Bakewell Tart (Derbyshire)
Banbury Cakes (Oxfordshire)
Cornish Pasties (Cornwall)
Devonshire Cream (Devonshire)
Irish Stew (Ireland)
Lancashire Hot Pot (Lancashire)
Melton Mowbray Pie (Leicestershire)
Stilton Cheese (Cambridgeshire)
Welsh Rarebit (Wales)
Yorkshire Pudding (Yorkshire)

POULTRY

Domesticated fowl such as chickens, turkeys, ducks, and geese are known as poultry. The cuts of meat from these birds are all labelled in the same way, and are shown in the following chart.

1. Neck
2. Wing
3. Thigh
4. Drumstick/Leg
5. Breast
6. Wishbone

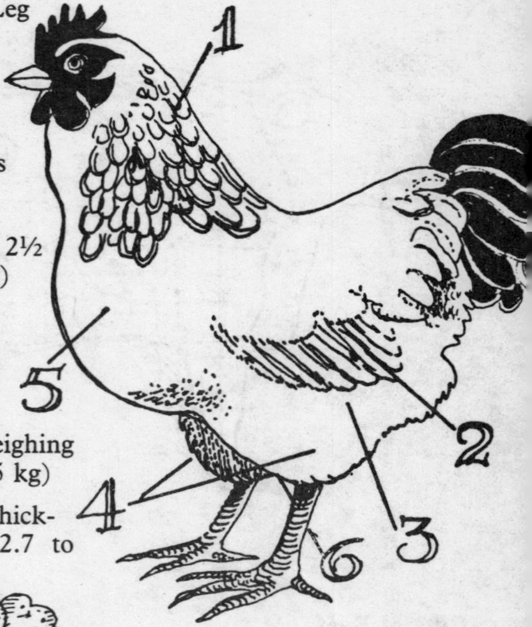

What is a . . .

Poussins—Young chickens weighing up to 2 lbs. (1 kg) each

Broilers—Young chickens 2½ to 3½ lbs (1.13–1.68 kg) in weight

Roasting chickens—Birds weighing 4 to 5 lbs (1.8–2.25 kg)

Boiling fowl—Chickens weighing from 6 to 8 lbs (2.7–3.15 kg)

Capons—Castrated male chickens weighing 6–8 lbs (2.7 to 3.15 kg)

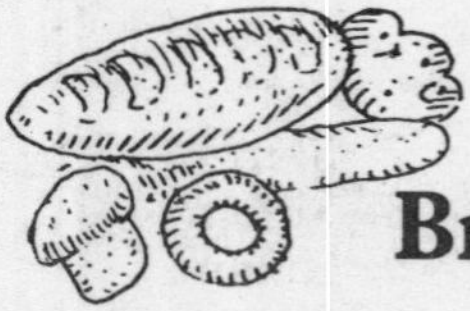

Bread

Bread is a universal food. It is made in many shapes and prepared in many ways. Below is a sampling of the traditional breads from around the world.

Origin	*Bread Name*
American	Sourdough, white bread
Armenian	Filo bread
Chinese	Dumpling, steamed buns
Danish	Pastries
English	Cottage loaf
Finnish	Flat bread

Origin	*Bread Name*
French	Croissant, baguette
German	Zwieback, Christmas stollen
Greek	Easter bread
Indian	Paratha, pooris
Irish	Soda bread
Italian	Twist bread, pizza
Japanese	Shina fu
Jewish	Bagel, challah
Mideastern	Pita bread
Mexican	Tortillas
Native American	Acorn bread, Navaho fried bread
Scottish	Baps, scones

Inventions

From tape measures to TVs, the many gadgets people use had to be invented by someone. Many fascinating facts can be found among the inventors and inventions.

Inventions A-Z

Invention	*Inventor*	*Year Patented*
Airplane with motor ('Flying Machine')	Orville Wright; Wilbur Wright	1906
Aspirin ('Acetylsalicylic Acid')	Hermann Dresser; Felix Hoffman	1889
Bakelite	Leo H. Beckeland	1907
Ball-point pen	John J. Loud	1888
Biro pen	Ladislao and Georg Biro	1938
'Cash Register and Indicator'	James Ritty; John Ritty	1879

Invention	*Inventor*	*Year Patented*
Celluloid	Alexander Parkes	1861
Cinema	Auguste and Louis Lumière	1895
Cosmetics (modern)	George Washington Carver	1925
Cotton gin	Eli Whitney	1794
Cylinder lock (Door lock)	Linus Yale, Jr.	1844
Diesel Engine	Rudolf Diesel	1898
Electric Razor ('Shaving Implement')	Jacob Schick	1928
Hovercraft	Sir Christopher Cockerell	1953
Frozen Foods (packaged)	Clarence Birdseye	1930
Icemaking Machine	John Gorrie	1851
Jet Engine	Sir Frank Whittle	1937
Laser	Arthur L. Schawlow; Charles H. Townes	1960
'Life Raft'	Frederick S. Allen	1881
Lift	Elisha G. Otis	1852
Locomotive	Richard Trevithick	1804
Matches (friction)	Alonso D. Phillips	1836
'Microphone'	Emile Berliner	1880
Motion Picture Projector	Thomas A. Edison	1892
'Motor Carriage'	Henry Ford	1901

Invention	*Inventor*	*Year Patented*
Navigable Balloon	J. Etienne; J. Montgolfier	1783
Nuclear Reactor	Enrico Fermi; Leo Szilard	1955
Nylon	Wallace H. Carothers	1937
Pasteurization	Louis Pasteur	1873
Phonograph	Thomas A. Edison	1877
Photography (on paper)	W. H. Fox Talbot	1835
Pneumatic Tyre	John Boyd Dunlop	1888
Radar	Sir Robert Watson Watt	1935
Refrigeration	Jacob Perkins	1834
Revolver	Samuel Colt	1836
Rocket Engine	Robert H. Goddard	1914
Rubber (Waterproof)	Charles Macintosh	1819
Safety Pin	Walter Hunt	1849
Sewing Machine	Elias Howe, Jr.	1846
'Speaking Telegraph'	Thomas A. Edison	1892
Spinning frame	Sir Richard Arkwright	1769
Steamboat	Robert Fulton	1811
Stethoscope	Rene Laennec	1819
Suspenders	Samuel Clemens (Mark Twain)	1871
Tape Measure	Alvin J. Fellows	1868
Telegraph Signs	Samuel F. B. Morse	1840
Telephone	Alexander Graham Bell	1876
Television	John Logie Baird	1926
Terylene	J. R. Whitfield and J. T. Dickson	1941

Invention	*Inventor*	*Year Patented*
Typewriter	C. Latham Sholes; Carlos Glidden; Samuel W. Soule	1868
Vacuum Cleaner	Ives W. McGaffey	1869
Videotape Recorder	Charles P. Ginsburg; Shelby Anderson, Jr.; Ray M. Dolby	1960
Vulcanized Rubber	Charles Goodyear	1844
Washing Machine	Chester Stone	1827
Wireless Telegraph	Guglielmo Marconi	1896
X-ray	Wilhelm Röntgen	1895
Zip fastener	Whitcomb Judson	1893

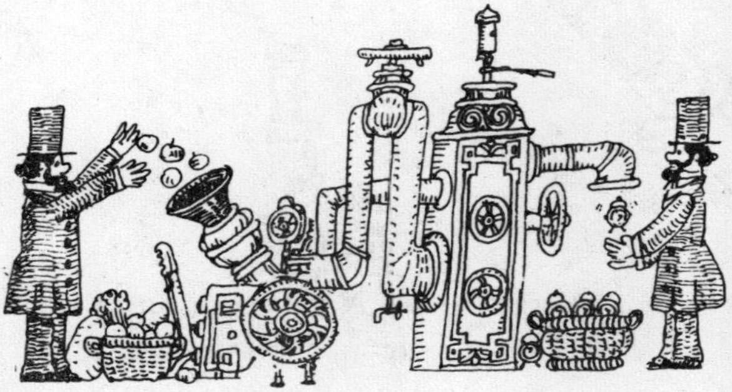

Medicine

Do you know how many bones are in your body? What kind of doctor is a cardiologist? What ancient people first performed surgery? These are some of the fascinating facts you can learn about in this chapter on Medicine.

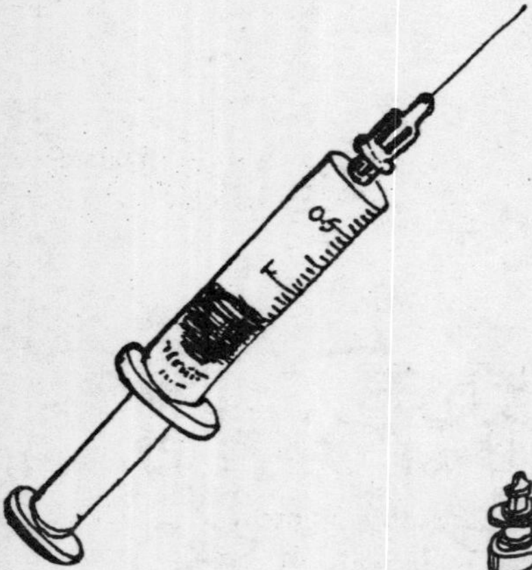

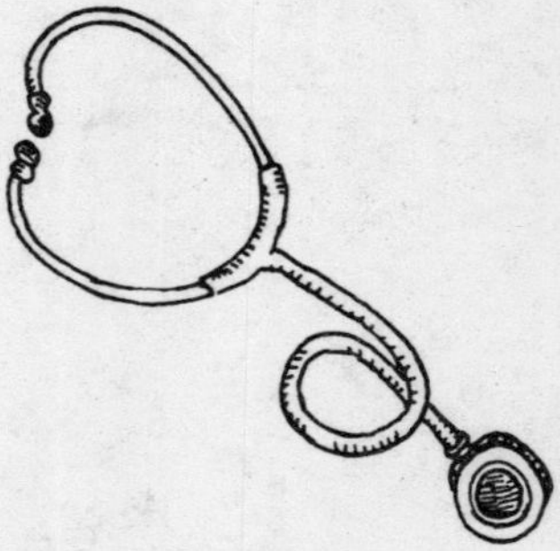

Medical Milestones

B.C.

2700 The Chinese emperor Shen-Nung is the first to use acupuncture.

1500 The Egyptians describe diseases and surgery on papyrus scrolls.

600 The Hebrews are the first to make laws for cleanliness and diet.

400 Hippocrates, the Greek physician known as the 'father of doctors,' writes an oath for doctors. By taking this oath, doctors promise to follow certain medical values and ethics.

A.D.

190 Galen of Greece, physician of the Roman Empire, writes about the functions of body organs. His system of medicine is followed for over a thousand years.

1590 Invention of the microscope by Dutch optician Zacharias Janssen.

1628 William Harvey of England describes how blood circulates.

1683 Dutch naturalist Anton van Leeuwenhoek is the first to see and describe bacteria through a microscope.

1796 Edward Jenner of England develops the first successful vaccination against smallpox.

1819 French doctor Rene Laennec invents the stethoscope.

1854 Florence Nightingale, an English nurse, starts the profession of trained nursing.

1859 French chemist Louis Pasteur is the first to write about the 'germ theory' of disease.

1864 Louis Pasteur discovers pasteurization, a process which kills harmful bacteria in liquids.

1865 Joseph Lister of England is the first to perform an antiseptic (germfree) operation.

1895 Discovery of X-rays by German physicist, Wilhelm Röntgen.

1900 Sigmund Freud, an Austrian doctor, founds modern psychoanalysis.

1921 First microsurgery (an operation using a microscope and miniature tools) is performed in an operation of the middle ear.

1928 Alexander Fleming of Scotland discovers penicillin.

1953 Beginning of cryogenics (super cold) in surgery with a successful operation performed by U.S. physician Henry Swan.

1954 Dr. Jonas Salk of the U.S. develops the polio vaccine.

1954 The first organ (kidney) transplant is performed at Peter Bent Brigham Hospital in Boston.

1967 South African doctor Christiaan Barnard performs the first human heart transplant.

1972 Beginning of the use of medicine in outer space, testing the effects of space travel on the human body.

1972 The CAT scan first shows clean pictures of cross sections of the body. (CAT stands for Computer Assisted Axial Tomography.)

1978 The world's first baby conceived in a test tube outside the mother's body is born in Oldham, England. Her name is Louise Joy Brown. Artificial skin is developed by Flow Laboratories, Inc., a biomedical company in Virginia.

1982 The first artificial heart is implanted in a human by surgeon, William Devries.

1983 More than three million artificial body parts are implanted in humans.

1984 The first electronic hearing system is implanted in a deaf person.

1984 The first computer system to produce artificial joint design is developed at the Hospital for Special Surgery in New York City.

Stories Behind Common Health Aids

ASPIRIN

The most widely-used pain killer in the world is aspirin. It was perfected by German researchers Felix Hoffman and Hermann Dresser in 1899. It was first sold under the trade name Bayer Aspirin in 1905 by prescription only, and in powder form. By 1915, tablets of aspirin were sold over the counter.

BAND-AIDS

The first adhesive bandages were made by Earl Dickson, an employee of Johnson & Johnson. He designed them for his wife who was prone to cuts and scrapes. The company liked these bandages, named them Band-Aids, and began selling them in 1921.

EYEGLASSES

The first people known to wear eyeglasses were the 13th-century Mongols. These eyeglasses were made of convex-shaped quartz with frames of tortoise shells. In the 1700s, Benjamin Franklin came up with the idea of combining far-sighted and near-sighted glasses into one pair of bifocal glasses. The first contact lenses were made in the 1880s, even though Leonardo da Vinci had thought of them as early as the 1500s.

THERMOMETER

The very first thermometer to measure heat was invented by Galileo. Santorio, a friend of Galileo, was inspired by Galileo's invention and invented the clinical thermometer to record body temperature. Today it is the most widely-used medical tool in the world.

TOOTH CLEANERS

The first known instrument to clean teeth was the toothpick. It was used as early as 3000 B.C. by the Sumerians who had toothpicks made of gold. The toothbrush may have been invented by the Chinese in the 15th century. The first toothbrushes used in Europe were said to be made by a London prisoner, William Addis, about 1770.

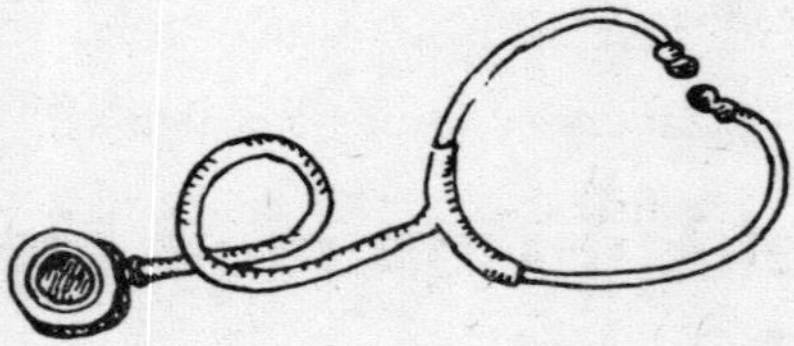

A Doctor Directory

Allergist—Treats allergies.

Anaesthetist—Puts patients to sleep before surgery.

Cardiologist—Treats heart ailments.

Dermatologist—Treats the skin and its diseases.

Endocrinologist—Treats the glands such as the thyroid and adrenal which secrete body hormones.

Gastroenterologist—Specializes in diseases and disorders of the digestive system.

Geriatrician—Treats diseases of old age.

Gynaecologist—Treats women's diseases.

Haematologist—Treats blood diseases.

Immunologist—Specializes in the body's defence system against infection and disease.

Obstetrician—A doctor who cares for women throughout pregnancy.

Ophthalmologist—Treats the eye and its diseases.

Orthodontist—A dentist who specializes in straightening teeth.

Orthopaedist—Treats disorders of bones and muscles.

Otolaryngologist—Treats ailments of the ear, nose and throat (ENT specialist).

Pathologist—Studies the cause, development, and manifestations of disease.

Paediatrician—Specializes in the care and treatment of infants and children.

Psychiatrist—Treats illnesses and disorders of the mind.

Radiologist—Uses X-rays for medical diagnosis.

Rheumatologist—Treats diseases of body joints.

Urologist—Treats the urinary tract of the body.

Body Facts

- There are more than 26 billion cells in a newborn baby.
- More than two-thirds of body weight is made up of fluids.
- There are over 650 muscles in the body, from the tiny ones that move the eyelids to the powerful ones that move the legs.
- The brain is the body's main control centre. Messages are sent from the brain to the body at a rate of 240 miles per hour.

- Some body reflexes are:
  Sneezing—which clears dirt from the nose,
  Coughing—which clears mucus from the throat,
  Yawning—which brings more oxygen to the lungs, and
  Shivering—which warms the body.
- The main organ of balance is in the inner ear.
- The skin is one of the body's most important parts. It weighs about 6 pounds, is waterproof, and helps protect the body from dirt and germs.
- It takes 24 hours for food to travel over 30 feet through your body.
- The eyes weigh 1½ ounces each. Both eyes move together. They are always in motion, even during sleep.
- Adults have 32 teeth. There are three kinds of teeth for chewing food: the incisors chop it, the canines tear it, and the molars grind it up.
- There are 206 bones in the body:
  Arm—32
  Leg—31
  Skull—29
  Spine—26
  Chest—25

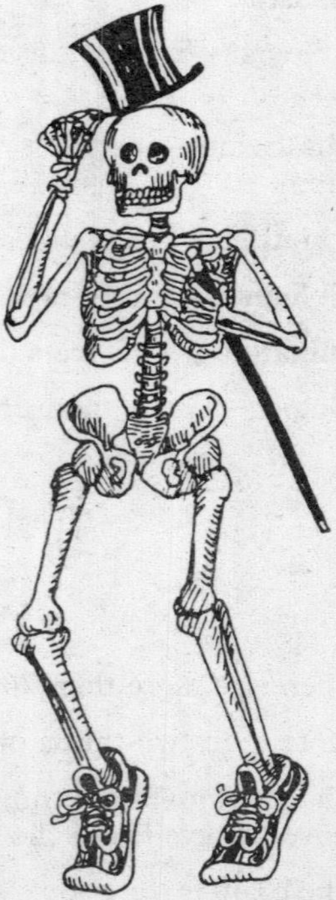

Money

Whether it's pocket money, or a job to earn it, money is a subject of interest to most kids. In this chapter you can learn about money from around the world, find out about the first paper money and coins, and discover whether you can visit 'money places' in London.

Paper Money

• The forerunner of paper money was leather money—pieces of white stag skin embellished with designs of water plants issued by Emperor Wu between 140 and 86 B.C.

• The first paper money was issued by Emperor Hein Tsung in China between A.D. 806 and 821.

• Leather money was issued in Europe and elsewhere, the last recorded instance was when some was issued by Chief Sitting Bull during a Red Indian uprising in 1875.

• The first bank note printed on paper in Europe was issued by the Bank of Sweden in 1661.

• The first notes issued in large denominations by the Bank of England were circulated in 1694. The design remained little changed until 1956.

• The first official issue of paper money in America was made in Massachusetts Bay in 1690. Such notes are termed 'colonial currency'.

• In 1923 in Germany the highest notes issued were for 100 thousand million marks (worth about £8 at the time). The highest denomination ever issued was printed in Hungary in 1946 with a face value of 20,000 million, million, million, million pengo.

• The highest denomination note in circulation in the USA is the $10,000 although it has not been printed since 1944.

Coins

• Coins were first struck in the 8th century B.C. Croesus, King of Lydia in Asia Minor (now Turkey) was the first to introduce pure gold coins.

• The first important gold coin of European commerce was the *bezant* which got its name from Byzantium (later Constantinople, now Istanbul). It remained the standard gold coin until the florin and ducat were coined in the 13th century.

• The word 'florin' is derived from Florence in Italy, and the coin was first minted in 1252.

• Edward VI introduced silver half-crowns, sixpences and threepences in 1551. The silver threepence ceased to be legal in 1971 and the silver sixpence in June 1980.

• The first guinea or sovereign was coined by Charles II in 1662. It was worth 20 shillings until 1717 when its value was changed to 21 shillings. It was called a guinea because it was made from gold from the Guinea Coast in West Africa.

• The modern British florin or two shillings (10p) first appeared in 1849.

• The official date when Britain changed to decimal currency was February 15, 1971.

• Most of the old coins have been withdrawn and officially have no value except to collectors. The old florin (10p) and shilling (5p) are still in circulation.

COIN	*DATE OF WITHDRAWAL*
Farthing	Dec. 1960
Half-penny	Aug. 1969
Half-crown	Jan. 1970
Threepenny piece (bronze)	Feb. 1971
Sixpence	June 1980

Dates of Introduction of New Decimal Coins

COIN	*DATE OF INTRODUCTION*
5 new pence	Apl. 1968
10 new pence	Apl. 1968
50 new pence	Oct. 1969
2 new pence	Feb. 1971
1 new penny	Feb. 1971
½ new penny	Feb. 1971
One pound	Apl. 1983

Money Around the World

BASIC UNITS OF MONEY IN 20 COUNTRIES

Country	*Unit*	*Country*	*Unit*
Austria	schilling	Jordan	dinar
Brazil	cruzeiro	Laos	kip
Canada	dollar	Mexico	peso
Denmark	krone	Morocco	dirham
France	franc	Netherlands	guilder
Great Britain	pound	Portugal	escudo
Greece	drachma	Russia	ruble
India	rupee	Spain	peseta
Italy	lira	West Germany	deutsche mark
Japan	yen	Zambia	kwacha

Forms of Money

Bonds are loans of money to governments or private companies. That money is returned to the bondholder with interest, after a certain amount of time.

Cheques are like letters to the bank. They tell the bank to give some of your money to someone as payment.

Credit cards are used by people who want to pay for something at a later time. The card is an identification card which is shown to the seller. The owner of the card signs a sales slip.

Money orders are issued by the Post Office. They can be bought for a small fee. They are most often used by people without bank accounts who want to send money safely through the mail. Money orders can be cashed at any Post Office.

Stocks are shares in a large company. When the company makes money the stockholder is paid a dividend.

Money Talk

The following are money terms and what they mean.

Bearish—Falling prices, particularly in the stock market. Bears are known to slap their enemies down.
Blue Chip—The most highly regarded industrial share. Originally an American gambling term derived from the highest value betting chips used in poker.
Bullish—Rising prices, particularly in the stock market. Bulls are known to toss their enemies up.
Dividend—Payments from a company's profits to its shareholders.
Gilt-edged—Government securities on which dividend payments are guaranteed.
Hush money—Money paid to keep someone quiet.
Kitty—A sum of money collected from a group of people to be used for a certain purpose.
Mad money—Extra money to be used frivolously.
Moneybags—A person with a great deal of money.
Money talks—Money influences people.
Piggybank—First named after the clay called pygg from which early Americans made coin banks. Later these clay coin banks were made into the shape of pigs.
Shares—The capital stock of a company.
Smart money—Money wisely invested.
Worth his salt—The Romans once paid their soldiers' salaries in salt. Today this term means a person is worth his wages.

American Money Slang

Money	—	bills, bread, dough, green, lettuce
$1	—	ace, bean, buck, one-spot, single
$5	—	fin, fiver
$10	—	sawbuck, ten-spot
$20	—	double sawback
$50	—	half a yard
$100	—	benji, C-note, yard
$500	—	five bills, five Cs, half a G
$1000	—	a grand, a G, a large

Money Places to Visit

The City of London is one of the great financial centres in the world. The headquarters of banks, the Stock Exchange where shares in businesses are bought and sold, insurance, and markets where the prices of many basic commodities are decided, are all located here.

It is possible to visit some of these, but the number of visitors is restricted, so it is advisable to enquire first. Advance booking is necessary in most cases.

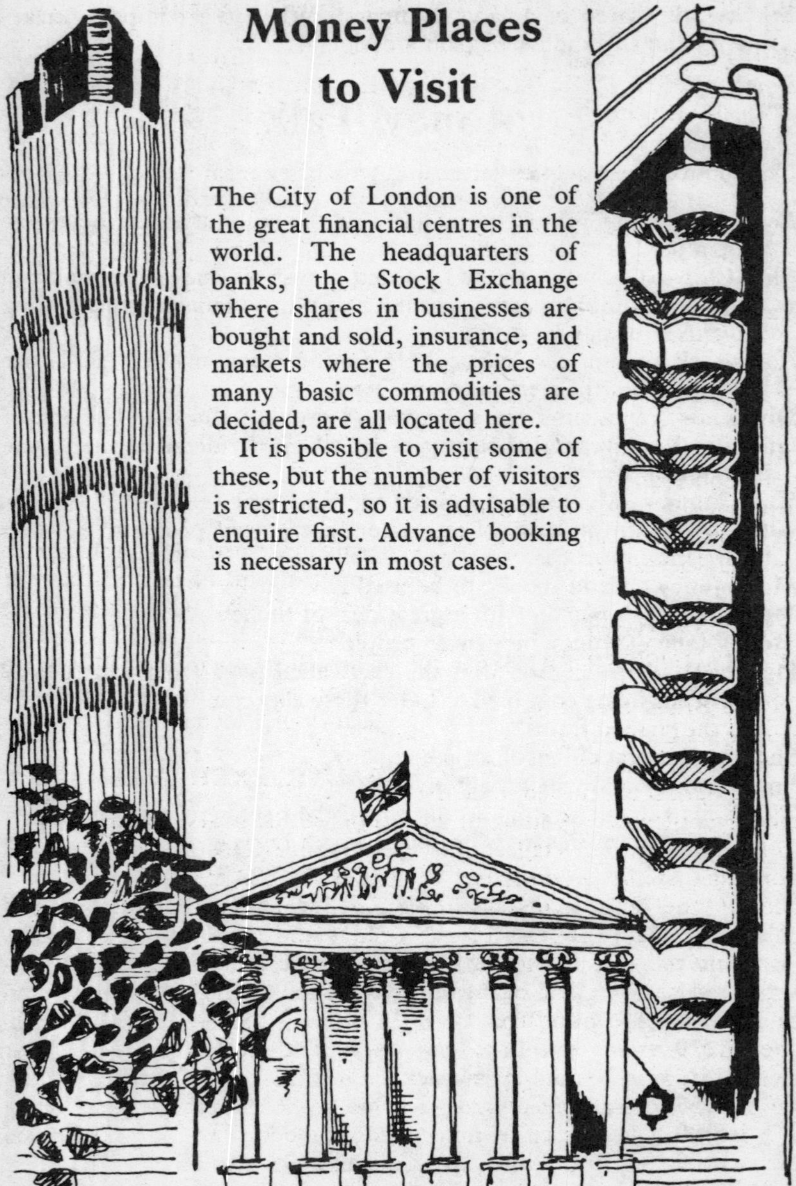

BANK OF ENGLAND

Threadneedle Street
London EC2R 8AH
(Tel: 01–601 4878)
Nationalised in 1946, the Bank of England keeps the main Government banking accounts, issues bank-notes, oversees the foreign exchange market, and advises the Government on money matters. Visits can be organised for groups of between 12 and 15 people if pre-booked well in advance. Tours last about 1½ hours and include visits to the Bank's Museum. Individual members of the public can go, but a letter of introduction from a bank manager is required and all visitors must be over 15 years of age.

THE NATIONAL WESTMINSTER BANK

25 Old Broad Street
London EC2N 1HQ.
(Tel: 01–920 5555)
600 ft high, it is believed to be the tallest cantilevered building in the world and is Britain's tallest office building. As the headquarters of one of the 'big four' clearing banks, its main interest for the visitor is the internal mail train and the sensational view of eight counties which can be seen (on a fine day) from the roof-top viewing gallery. Visits last 1 hour and must be pre-arranged through a local Nat-West Branch Manager.

THE STOCK EXCHANGE

Old Broad Street
London EC2N 1HP
(Tel: 01–588 2355)
The gallery is open from 9.45 A.M. to 3.15 P.M. on weekdays, except Saturday. In addition there are 6 'set visits' at 10 A.M., 10.30 A.M. and thereafter at every half-hour until 2.30 P.M. A 10-minute film is shown and there is a souvenir shop to visit.

LLOYDS OF LONDON

Leadenhall Street
London
(Tel: 01–623 7100 ex. 3733)
The new building has been compared to an oil rig transported from the North Sea, but whatever the criticism it is the most sensational building in London. The gallery opens from 10 A.M. to 4 P.M. and a museum shows the history of Lloyds.

BALTIC EXCHANGE

14 – 20 St. Mary Axe
London EC3A 8BU
(Tel: 01–623 5501)
The business here is the hiring of ships and the shipping of goods. Visits can be arranged on Wednesdays, Thursdays and Fridays at 11.30 A.M. and 12.30 P.M. The programme lasts 1 hour and consists of a lecture, a film and a view of the trading floor. No students below sixth form level are admitted.

METAL EXCHANGE

Plantation House,
Fenchurch Street
London EC3M 3AP
(Tel: 01–626 1828)
Here the daily price of metals is decided in hectic trading. Visits are timed for 12 noon when a 20-minute film is shown. Students must be at 'A' level age and booking well in advance is necessary.

THE ROYAL EXCHANGE

Threadneedle Street and Cornhill,
London EC3V 3PJ
(Tel: 01–623 0444 ex 262/265)
A building of classical style built in the 1840s and standing adjacent to the Mansion House, the Royal Exchange was originally used as a stock exchange and Lloyds shipping insurance for a time. The central courtyard now houses an inner building used by the London International Financial Futures Exchange. The Public Gallery is open from 11.30 A.M. to 1.45 P.M. on business days. Group educational visits at other times can be arranged.

THE ROYAL MINT

Llantrisant, S. Wales
All our coins, as well as those for over 65 other countries, are minted here, but for security reasons visits are no longer possible.

Museums

It would take five years if you visited a different museum in Great Britain everyday but here are just a selection to whet your appetite.

NATIONAL MUSEUMS

British Museum
Great Russell Street,
London WC1B 3DG.
(Tel: 01–635 1555)
One of the greatest collections of antiquities in the world, including the ever popular Eygptian mummies.

Victoria and Albert Museum
Cromwell Road, South Kensington
London SW7 2RL.
(Tel: 01–589 6371)
One of the world's greatest collections of the decorative and fine arts, including Tippoo's Tiger.

Museum of London
London Wall, EC2Y 5HN.
(Tel: 01–600 3699)
250,000 years of London History, including the Great Fire and the Lord Mayor's State Coach.

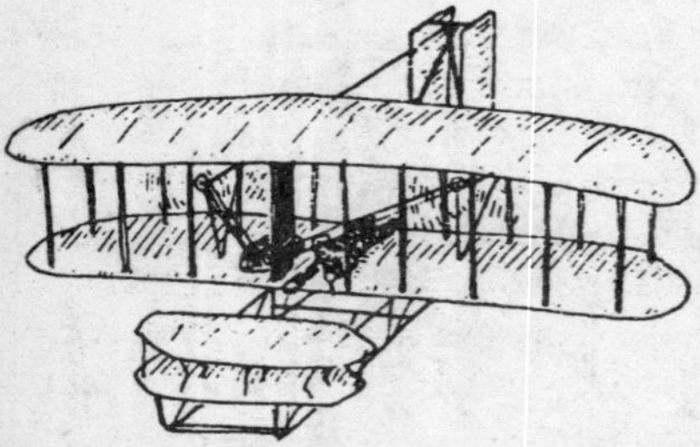

Science Museum
Exhibition Road,
South Kensington, SW7 2DD.
(Tel: 01–589 3456)
Early steam engines, a real *Apollo 10* space capsule, and Exploration Galleries.

Natural History Museum
Cromwell Road,
South Kensington, SW7 5BD.
(Tel: 01–589 6323)
Fossils, man and, of course, dinosaurs, as well as the recorded songs of nearly 50 British birds.

Geological Museum
Exhibition Road, South Kensington, London, SW2 2DE
(Tel: 01–589–3444)
The history of the Earth and the regional geology of Britain, as well as the famous gemstone collection.

The Tate Gallery
Millbank, London, SW1P 4RG
(Tel: 01–821–7128)
The national collection of British painting and Modern Art.

The National Gallery
Trafalgar Square, London, WC2N 5DN
(Tel: 01–839–3526)
The national collection of European painting from c. 1200 to 1900.

Museum of Mankind
6, Burlington Gardens, London W1X 2EX
(Tel: 01–437 2224)
Dramatic masks and carvings and objects of all sorts showing the art of other cultures from distant lands.

National Portrait Gallery
St Martin's Place, Trafalgar Square, London, WC2H 0HE
(Tel: 01–930 1552)
Portraits of the famous and infamous in British history.

CHILDHOOD

Museum of Childhood
38 High Street, Edinburgh, EH1 1TG.
(Tel: 031–225–2424)
Toys from 1880s to 1950s and 40,000 other exhibits about childhood.

Bethnal Green Museum of Childhood
Cambridge Heath Road
London, E2 9PA.
(Tel: 01–980 2415)
Over 1,000 dolls and many dolls houses, as well as toys, games and clothes.

Windsor Castle
Windsor, Berks.
(Tel: Windsor (0753) 868286)
Queen Mary's dolls' house—a perfect replica of a 20th-century house complete with tiny models of the contents made by craftsmen.

London Toy and Model Museum
23 Craven Hill, London, W2
(Tel: 01–262 9450/7905)
Mechanical toys and models galore.

Sudbury Hall Mansion,
Sudbury, Derbyshire
(Tel: (028 378) 305)
A mock chimney to climb, a mousehole peep-show and things to do in every room.

SCENES FROM HISTORY

Geffrye Museum
Kingsland Rd., Shoreditch
London E2 8EA.
(Tel: 01–739 8368)
A vivid display of rooms from 1600 to 1939.

Castle Museum
York, YO1 1RY.
(Tel: York (0904) 53611)
Reconstructed streets and period shops and rooms.

Jorvik Viking Centre,
Coppergate, York, YO1 1NT.
(Tel: York (0904) 643211)
A Viking street has been recreated, even down to authentic sounds and smells.

Weald and Downland Open Air Museum, Singleton,
Nr. Chichester, W. Sussex.
(Tel: Singleton (024 363) 348)
Real medieval buildings have been rescued and reconstructed

here, including a blacksmith's forge and village school.

The Royal Pavilion, Brighton
(Tel: (0273) 603005)
The seaside palace of the Prince Regent (George IV) containing some of the most dazzling and magnificent interiors in the world.

Roman Palace,
Salthill Road, Fishbourne, Nr. Chichester, W. Sussex
(Tel: 0243 785421)
The huge palace of King Cogidubnus with wonderfully mosaic floors and a good little museum.

TRANSPORT

London Transport Museum
Covent Garden, London WC2.
(Tel: 01–379 6344)
Everything connected with London Transport including old buses, trams and trolley buses.

National Motor Museum
Palace House, Beaulieu, Hants.
(Tel: Beaulieu (0590) 612345)
Marvellous old cars and motor cycles telling the story of motoring from 1895 to modern times.

National Railway Museum
Leeman Road, York.
(Tel: York (0904) 21261)
A feast for railway enthusiasts, including Queen Victoria's coach of 1869 and the record-breaking *Mallard* Locomotive.

ARMED SERVICES

Cabinet War Rooms
Clive Steps, King Charles Street, London SW1A 2AQ
(Tel: 01–930 6961)
Nineteen historic rooms in a deep basement shelter where Winston Churchill and the War cabinet and the chiefs of staff could carry on thier work protected against air attack.

National Maritime Museum
Romney Road, Greenwich, SE10 9NF.
(Tel: 01–858 4422)
Lovely models of ships, and displays devoted to famous sailors.

Imperial War Museum
Lambeth Road,
London, SE1 6H2.
(Tel: 01–735 8922)
Weapons and equipment from past wars, and special displays.

National Army Museum
Royal Hospital Road,
London, SW3 4HT.
(Tel: 01–730 0717)
Five centuries of British Army history.

Royal Air Force Museum
Hendon, NW9 5LL.
(Tel: 01–205 2266)
The remarkable history of aviation and the R.A.F.

FOR SPECIALISTS

HMS *Belfast*
Symons Wharf, Vine Lane,
London SE1 2JH.
(Tel: 01–407 6434)
Explore a real World War II cruiser!

Quarry Bank Mill
Styal, Cheshire.
(Tel: Wilmslow (0625) 527468)
A working Georgian cotton mill.

Chatterley Whitfield Mining Museum
Tunstall ST6 8UN
(Tel: (0782) 813337)
Visit a mine 700 ft. below ground!

Potter's Museum of Curiosity
6 High Street, Arundel,
W. Sussex.
(Tel: Arundel (0903) 882420)
An amazing collection, famous for its tableaux of stuffed birds and animals, such as 'the kitten's tea party'.

Mechanical Music and Doll Collection
Church Road, Portfield,
Chichester, W. Sussex.
(Tel: Chichester (0243) 785421)
A musical treat from the past.

Museum of Costume
Assembly Rooms, Bath, Avon.
(Tel: Bath (0225) 6111 ext. 327)
A pageant of clothes from 17th to 20th century.

Ironbridge Gorge Museum
Ironbridge, Telford,
Shropshire, TF8 7AW
(Tel. (095 245) 3522)
A unique series of industrial monuments, including working exhibits.

Fox Talbot Museum
Lacock, Wilts.
(Tel: Lacock (024 973) 459)
The history of photography displayed in the home of the man who first made prints on silver chloride paper.

National Postal Museum
King Edward Building, King Edward Street, London, EC1 1LP
(Tel: 01–930 1552)
A haven for every stamp collector and postal historian.

Baden-Powell Museum
Baden-Powell House, Queen's Gate, London, SW7 5JS
(Tel: 01–584 7030)
Momentoes of Baden-Powell that every Boy Scout should see.

Tower of London
Tower Hill, London, EC3N 4AB
(Tel: 01–709 0765)
Not only one of Europe's great ancient fortresses byt the home of the world's finest collection of arms and armour – not forgetting the Crown Jewels.

Music

Rock, Pop, Reggae, Folk, Country, Jazz, Swing. If you like music, these pages will 'sing' with things you'll want to know.

Music Trivia

1. What is the earliest known written music?
ANSWER: An Assyrian clay tablet inscribed with a form of musical notation has been found dating from 1800 B.C.
2. How did the English horn get its name?
ANSWER: It is a type of oboe with a bulbous end and a curved mouth piece, sometimes called a cor anglais. It has been suggested that as it has an angled mouth piece the French called it *angle* which sounded like *anglais* (English) and the words became confused.
3. What composer has written the most million-selling singles in pop music?
ANSWER: Paul McCartney.
4. What is the most frequently sung song in the world?
ANSWER: 'Happy Birthday to You' written by the American sisters Patty and Mildred Hill in 1893.
5. Who was the youngest musical progeny?
ANSWER: Yehudi Menuhin, the American violinist, appeared as a soloist with the San Francisco Symphony Orchestra at the age of seven. Mozart made his first professional tour through Europe when he was six years old. But the youngest known is William Crotch, who gave his first public organ recital in Norwich in 1778 when he was only three years old.
6. Who won the most Grammy Awards (given for artistic achievement in the recording field) in one year?
ANSWER: Michael Jackson, who won 8 for the year 1983.
7. Who was the first recording artist to win a gold record?
ANSWER: Perry Como in 1958 for his song 'Catch A Falling Star'.
8. Who is the best-selling classical pianist in recording history?
ANSWER: Polish-born Artur Rubinstein, who first played in the U.S. in 1906. He has become one of the most widely-loved U.S. concert pianists selling more than 10 million of his 200 recordings.
9. What is the biggest and most powerful musical instrument?
ANSWER: The pipe organ. The largest pipe organ on record is the Auditorium Organ in Atlantic City, New Jersey, which has 33,112 pipes and the volume of 25 brass bands.
10. What orchestra has given more concerts than any other in the world?
ANSWER: The New York Philharmonic began playing in 1842. In 1982 it played its 10,000th concert and has performed over a thousand more since then.

11. Who was the most famous violin maker in history?
ANSWER: Antonio Stradivarius (1644–1737) of Italy. No one has been able to duplicate the sound of his violins. It is not known whether his formula for varnish, the sap applied to the wood, or the wood itself is the secret to his violins. Today, a Stradivarius violin is worth over $450,000.
12. What was the first opera ever composed?
ANSWER: *Dafne* by Jacopo Peri of Florence, Italy in 1597.
13. Which record is said to have sold the most?
ANSWER: 'White Christmas' by Irving Berlin. The Bing Crosby recording has sold 25,000,000 copies and more than 100 million have sold in other versions.
14. Where is the capital of jazz in the United States?
ANSWER: New Orleans, Louisiana.
15. What was the first Broadway musical written and produced by blacks?
ANSWER: *Shuffle Along* by Eubie Blake and Nobel Sissle in 1921.
16. What music is played when the president of the U.S. appears in public?
ANSWER: 'Hail to the Chief.'
17. What was the first music video nominated for an Academy Award (given for excellence in motion pictures)?
ANSWER: *Thriller* by Michael Jackson.
18. Who was the most successful music group ever?
ANSWER: The Beatles sold over a hundred million singles and a hundred million albums.
19. What was the greatest selling classical record?
ANSWER: *Switched-on Bach* by Walter Carlos (1968) featuring many of Bach's best known works played on the Moog Synthesizer.
20. What is the top-selling British single of all time?
ANSWER: 'Feed the World—Do They Know It's Christmas', written and produced by Bob Geldorf and Midge Ure. Issued in December 1984 it has sold 4 million world-wide. It was performed by 41 artists, and all the profits went to the Ethiopian Famine Relief Fund. The previous best was Paul McCartney's 'Mull of Kintyre' which sold 2½ million.
21. What is the largest audience there has ever been for a pop concert?
ANSWER: It is estimated that Bob Geldorf's 'Live Aid Concert' on July 13, 1985 was watched by 2,000 million viewers on TV worldwide.

Gold Record Chart

This is a list of the number of records that must be sold to win a gold record in countries around the world.

Country	*Number of Singles*	*Country*	*Number of Singles*
Australia	50,000	Italy	1,000,000
Austria	100,000	The Netherlands	100,000
Canada	75,000	Poland	250,000
Denmark	50,000	Spain	100,000
Finland	10,000	Sweden	100,000
France	500,000	United Kingdom	500,000
Hungary	100,000	U.S.A.	1,000,000
Ireland	100,000	West Germany	1,000,000

Musical Notes

Five Musicians Who Influenced Popular Music

Bill Haley and His Comets—Rock 'n' Roll
Woody Guthrie—Folk Music
Ray Charles—Rhythm and Blues
Dave Brubeck—Modern Progressive Jazz
Bob Marley—Reggae Music

Five Funny Song Titles

'The Purple People Eater'—1958
'Does Your Chewing Gum Lose Its Flavor on the Bedpost Overnight?'—1961
'The Monster Mash'—1962
'Itsy Bitsy Tennie Weenie Yellow Polka Dot Bikini'—1960
'A Boy Named Sue'—1968

Five Grammy Award-Winning 'Records of the Year'

1980 'Sailing,' sung by Christopher Cross
1981 'Bette Davis Eyes,' sung by Kim Carnes
1982 'Rosanna,' sung by Toto
1983 'Beat It,' sung by Michael Jackson
1984 'What's Love Got to Do with It,' sung by Tina Turner

Top Five Performers with the Most Pop Hits (1953–1983)

Elvis Presley
The Beatles
James Brown
Pat Boone
Fats Domino

Five Longest Running West End musicals

1. Jesus Christ Superstar
2. Oliver
3. Salad Days
4. Choo-Chin-Chow
5. Charlie Girl

Five Musical Groups with Animal Names

The Beatles
The Byrds
The Eagles
The Monkees
The Turtles

'Musical of the Year Awards'

1981 — Cats
1982 — Poppy
1983 — Blood Brothers
1984 — 42nd Street
1985 — Me and My Girl

Five Kings of Music

'The King'—Elvis Presley
'King of Swing'—Benny Goodman
'King of Ragtime'—Scott Joplin
'King of Mountain Music'—Roy Acuff
'King of the Twelve-String Guitar'—Leadbelly (Huddie Ledbetter)

Five Queens of Music

'Queen of Soul'—Aretha Franklin
'Queen of the Blues'—Bessie Smith
'Queen of Country Music'—Mother Maybelle Carter
'Queen of Folk Music'—Joan Baez
'Queen of Rock'—Janis Joplin

Five Firsts in Rock 'n' Roll

- The first to use the term rock 'n' roll was Alan Freed, a disc jockey from Cleveland. In 1952 he changed the name of his radio show to 'Morning Rock 'n' Roll House Party'.
- The first rock 'n' roll hit in the U.S. was 'Sh-Boom (Life Would Be A Dream)' by the Chords. It was recorded in 1954.
- The first rock film was *Blackboard Jungle*. This 1955 movie featured the hit song 'Rock Around the Clock' by Bill Haley and His Comets.
- The first to win a Gold Record for a rock 'n' roll single was Elvis Presley for his 1958 hit 'Hard Headed Woman'.
- The first Broadway rock musical was *Hair* which opened in 1968.

Five Kinds of Songs

Aria—A song with an instrumental accompaniment. Arias appear most commonly in operas.
Ballad—A folk song that tells a story.
Carol—A traditional song heard at Christmastime or on other holidays.
Round/Canon—A song in which all parts and voices have the same melody, each starting at a different time (e.g., 'Row Row Row Your Boat . . .').
Shanty—A song sung by sailors in earlier times to help them keep a rhythm as they worked.

Five Song Titles That Became Popular Sayings

'The Times They Are A-Changin',' Bob Dylan
'Give Peace A Chance,' John Lennon and Paul McCartney
'Say It Loud "I'm Black and I'm Proud",' James Brown
'You Are The Sunshine of My Life,' Stevie Wonder
'I Can't Get No Satisfaction,' Mick Jagger and Keith Richards

Five Kinds of Rock Music

Music	*Examples of Musicians*
Heavy Metal (Hard Rock)	Van Halen

New Wave	The Pretenders
Pop Rock	Olivia Newton-John
Punk	The Clash
Country Rock	The Stray Cats

Five Kinds of Jazz Music

Music	***Examples of Musicians***
Boogie Woogie	Jelly Roll Morton
Blues	Bessie Smith
Dixieland	The Preservation Hall Band
Modern	Miles Davis
Ragtime	Scott Joplin

Five Kinds of Country Music

Music	***Examples of Musicians***
Bluegrass	Bill Monroe
Cajun	Doug Kershaw
Country and Western	Hank Williams
Country Gospel	The Oak Ridge Boys
Western Swing	Bob Wills and the Texas Playboys

Classical Musical Notes

Five Music Professions

A composer writes music.
A conductor directs the performances of a chorus, band or orchestra.

A performer either plays an instrument or works as a solo or group artist.
A teacher works in a school or gives private lessons.
A tuner tunes musical instruments.

Five Forms of Classical Music

Ballet—A story danced to music, usually with scenery and costumes.
Concerto—A work for one or more solo instruments and orchestra.
Opera—A play or story that is sung and acted. An opera is usually staged with costumes, scenery, a chorus, and an orchestra.
Oratorio—A religious story put to music and usually performed by a chorus without scenery and costumes.
Symphony—A long musical composition for orchestra, usually in several movements.

Five Great Composers for Young People

Robert Schumann, a German who lived in the 1800s, was one of the first to write piano pieces for children. Among his works are 'Album for the Young' and 'Scenes from Childhood.'

Peter Ilyich Tchaikovsky was a Russian composer who lived from 1840 to 1893. He composed the music for *The Nutcracker*, a ballet loved by children.

Johannes Brahms, 19th-century German composer, wrote a now-famous lullaby, which has been sung by parents to babies for over a hundred years.

Sergei Prokofiev, who lived in Russia from 1891–1953, composed *Peter and the Wolf*, a classic favourite.

Benjamin Britten, an English 20th century composer, who wrote *Let's Make an Opera* and *Noye's Fludde*.

Five Notable Music Festivals

The Aldeburgh Festival in Suffolk, founded by Benjamin Britten and Peter Pears, is famous for its performance of contemporary British music.

The Bayreuth Festival is held in Bayreuth, Germany every July and August. The festival is dedicated to the music of Richard Wagner's operas.

The Edinburgh Festival is known for the variety of its music. It presents operas, ballets, and concerts every year from late August into September.

The Salzburg Festival in Salzburg, Austria is dedicated to the music of Mozart although other composers' works are included in the festival. It runs from late July through August every year.

The Three Choirs Festival is a choral festival dating from 1724 and is held annually in turn at Gloucester, Worcester and Hereford Cathedrals.

Five Famous National Anthems

- 'God Save the Queen', the royal anthem of Great Britain, is called the 'anthem of anthems.' Its melody is one of the most popular tunes in the world. Germany, Denmark, Sweden, Switzerland, and the U.S. all have national songs written to its tune. 'My Country 'tis of Thee' is the American national song which is sung to this melody.

- The national anthem of Austria is considered to be one of the most beautiful. 'Got Erhaltz' (May God Save) was composed by the great Austrian composer, Joseph Haydn.

- 'The Marseillaise' is the national anthem of France. Next to 'God Save the Queen,' it is the best-known national anthem. It was written by Claude Joseph Rouget de Lisle, a loyal subject of King Louis XVI. However, it was later used against the king as the song of the revolutionaries. In 1795 it became the official anthem of France.

- The words to 'The Star-spangled Banner' were written by Francis Scott Key in 1814 when he watched the British bomb Fort McHenry near Baltimore. It was not until 117 years later in 1931 that a law was passed making 'The Star-spangled Banner' the National Anthem of the U.S.

- The tiny country of Vatican City has an anthem. It is called the 'Marcia Pontificale' and was composed by Charles Gounod for Pope Pius IX in 1846. It became the official papal anthem in 1949.

The Orchestra

The orchestra is made up of four families of musical instruments. There are usually about 100 instruments in a symphony orchestra.

STRING INSTRUMENTS

About two-thirds of the orchestra is made up of instruments in the string family. The sounds of these instruments are made by drawing a bow across the strings or by plucking them.

VIOLIN

A four-stringed instrument, it is the smallest instrument in this family. Violins are the largest group of instruments in the orchestra; about thirty-six are in a standard orchestra.

VIOLA

An instrument like the violin, the viola is only one-seventh larger in size. The tone of the viola is lower than the violin. There are usually eight to ten violas in an orchestra.

CELLO

Twice the size of the viola, the cello is held between the knees. Its tone is eight notes (an octave) lower than the viola and there are usually ten to twelve cellos in an orchestra.

DOUBLE-BASS

The largest stringed instrument, it stands six feet tall. The player stands or sits on a high stool to play it. There are eight to ten in an orchestra.

HARP

The oldest instrument in the string section, the harp is also the only stringed instrument not in the violin family. Instead of four strings it has forty-seven, and it has seven pedals. The harp is not always played in an orchestra.

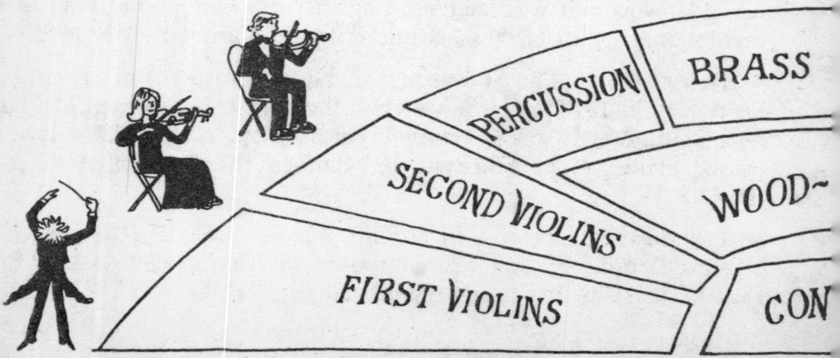

SEATING PLAN OF A

WOODWIND INSTRUMENTS

These instruments were named because they were originally made of wood and played by blowing wind into them. Today, they are still played in the same manner but many are made of metal rather than of wood. The notes are produced by pressing on the keys of the instrument.

FLUTE
This instrument is about two feet long and is held horizontally when played. The tones are made by pressing keys with the fingers. There are three in an orchestra.

PICCOLO
This instrument is a half-size flute that plays notes higher than the flute. There is one in an orchestra.

OBOE
A two-foot-long instrument, it is held vertically when played. The oboe is a double-reed instrument, meaning it has a mouthpiece made of two pieces of cane wood tied around a small tube. There are three in an orchestra.

ENGLISH HORN
A kind of oboe, this instrument is five notes lower and is one-and-a-half times the size of an oboe. There is one English horn player in an orchestra.

CLARINET
This is a single-reed instrument. There are three in an orchestra.

BASS CLARINET
Twice as large as a clarinet, this instrument plays eight notes lower. It is used occasionally in an orchestra.

BASSOON
An eight-foot-long instrument, it is doubled over to make it easier to handle. There are two in an orchestra.

DOUBLE BASSOON/ CONTRA BASSOON
This instrument is sixteen feet long but doubled four times to make it shorter. It plays the lowest notes of the woodwind instruments. There is one double bassoon player in an orchestra.

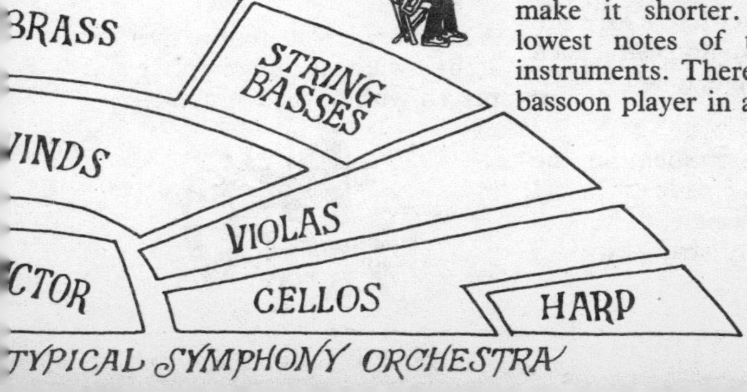

BRASS INSTRUMENTS

All of the instruments in this family are made of metal. They are blown to make music.

TRUMPET
This instrument is played by pressing three valves. The tube of a trumpet is eight feet long but is coiled around so the instrument is shorter and easier to handle. There are four trumpet players in an orchestra.

FRENCH HORN
There are three valves in a French horn which are pressed to produce different tones. The tube of this instrument is sixteen feet long and coiled around to make it manageable. There are three French horn players in an orchestra.

TROMBONE
This instrument has no valves.

The tones are produced by moving the slide back and forth while blowing into the instrument. A standard orchestra has three trombones.

TUBA
The heaviest and largest of brass instruments, its mouthpiece covers the mouth of most players. If the tube of this instrument were uncoiled it would stretch five feet. The tone, made by pressing valves, is very low. There is one tuba player in an orchestra.

PERCUSSION INSTRUMENTS

DRUMS
Snare drums are 16 inches across, the smallest in the drum family. Bass drums are four times larger than the snare. Kettle drums look like enormous kettles. There are three to four in an orchestra, each producing different tones.

TRIANGLE
The simplest instrument in the orchestra, it is made of steel shaped into a triangle. It tinkles like a bell when struck with a metal rod.

CYMBALS
Two brass plates which are clapped together to make a crashing sound.

GONG
A large brass plate four to five feet across, which is hung in place and played with a wooden mallet.

PEOPLE WHO ARE IMPORTANT TO THE ORCHESTRA

- **The composer** writes the music the orchestra plays. The parts for all the various instruments are written by the composer.
- **The conductor** interprets the music and directs the performance of the orchestra. The conductor must be able to read all the musical parts at once.
- **The leader of the orchestra** is the first violinist and is the lead musician in the orchestra. He helps the conductor train and rehearse the musicians in the orchestra.
- **The copyist** makes the music for each member of the orchestra to read.
- **The librarian** is responsible for preparing and setting out the music for each member of the orchestra.
- **The manager and his assistants** make the arrangements for the performances of the orchestra, including scheduling performance dates and making all travel and hotel arrangements for the orchestra when it travels.

Ten Italian Musical Terms

1. **A capella** (ah cah-pel' lah)—Unaccompanied choral singing.
2. **Adagio** (ah-dah' jo)—Slowly.
3. **Allegro** (ah-lay' groh)—Fast and lively.
4. **Crescendo** (creh-shen' doh)—Growing louder.
5. **Dimuendo** (dim-u-en-do)—Gradually growing softer.
6. **Forte** (for' tay)—Loud.
7. **Largo** (lar' goh)—Very slow.
8. **Legato** (lay-gah' toh)—Smooth and connected. To be played with no interruptions between notes.
9. **Staccato** (stah-cah' toh)—Sharply detached, one note from another.
10. **Tutti** (toot' ee)—The part of a composition in which all the instruments or voices perform together.

Milestones in Recording History

1877 Thomas Alva Edison of New Jersey first recorded sound on December 6. The tune he recorded was 'Mary had a little lamb'.
1888 The first popular artist to make a recording was 12-year-old Joseph Hoffman, a pianist in America.
1892 First British commercial recording on cylinder by the London Phonograph Co.
1897 Discs made their first appearance in Britain, released by the Gramophone Co.
1903 First 'unbreakable' record was made by Nicole Freres. He made it out of cardboard covered in shellac.
1926 The *Melody Maker* first published in Britain.
1948 First L.P. 78 record made by Columbia in America.
1949 First 45-rpm record made by RCA in America.
1950 First L.P. released in Britain by Decca.
1952 EMI released first 45-rpm record in Britain.
1954 Tape cartridges were invented by George Eash, a Los Angeles engineer.
1957–64 Argo issued the complete works of Shakespeare on 137 L.P.s. This is, to date, the largest recording project.
1960 First Pop Record Sales Charts of the Top 50 published in the UK by *Record Retailer* (*Music Weekly*). Earlier charts were produced but the method of collecting data was less reliable.
1963 Philips' cartridge (cassette) launched.
1964 'Top of the Pops' first broadcast on BBC TV on January 1.
1979 First compact disc demonstrated to the Press by Philips in Holland.
1983 European launch of compact disc.

National Instruments Around the World

Instrument	*Country of origin*	*Instrument*	*Country of origin*
1. Alpenhorn	Switzerland	6. Marimba	Guatemala
2. Bagpipe	Scotland	7. Sitar	India
3. Balalaika	Russia	8. Spike Fiddle	Thailand
4. Cimbalon	Hungary	9. Steel Drums	West Indies
5. Gusla	Yugoslavia	10. Trompong	Bali

People

The people in this chapter are famous; heroes who have overcome handicaps or those who have said unforgettable things. Some are the subjects of legends.

People Who Conquered Handicaps and Achieved Greatness

Sequoya

Sequoya was born in a Cherokee village in Tennessee in 1775. At a very early age Sequoya lost the use of one of his legs. His lameness prevented him from running and hunting with the other young braves, so he decided to spend his time drawing and painting. His drawings expressed his ideas. Soon he became interested in the way European settlers expressed their ideas—with written words or 'talking leaves'. Sequoya decided to dedicate his life to making a written system of communication for his people. After years of difficult and often discouraging work, he invented an alphabet of symbols known as 'syllabary.' Sequoya was able to teach his entire tribe to use the syllabary. As a result, the Cherokees were the first native Americans to read and write their language.

Louis Braille

When he was just 15 years old and blind, Louis Braille invented a system of writing which has been used by millions of blind people the world over. Louis was born in France in 1809 with normal eyesight. But when he was 3 years old he accidentally punctured one of his eyes. Infection set in and in a short time he lost the sight in both eyes. At the age of 13 he was attending a special school for the blind when he learned about a system called 'night writing'. It was meant for the blind but proved to be a cumbersome and difficult system. Louis was fascinated with the idea of inventing a writing system the blind could read. He worked on his idea for two years, after which he had developed the raised dot system called Braille.

Thomas Edison

Thomas Edison is known to most people as the inventor of the light bulb, phonograph, and the motion picture projector. However, what is not so widely known are the difficult years of his life when he was thought to be a slow learner. Edison was born in Ohio in 1847. Because of sickness and many family moves he did not enter school until he was 8 years old. His teachers were extremely frustrated with Thomas. They told his mother that he was a dreamer and could not learn. Thomas was taken out of school after a very short time and that was the only formal schooling he ever had. School was a painful experience for Thomas. His parents had faith in him, however, and his mother took up the task of teaching him. He was, as she thought, extremely bright. By the age of 10 he was spending hours in his basement doing scientific experiments. Edison grew up to be called 'the genius of his time'. His inventions have affected the lives of people all over the world.

Ludwig van Beethoven

Born at Bonn in West Germany in 1770, young Beethoven had a miserable childhood. His father was often drunk and was ruthless in his determination to exploit his son, who was giving public performances by the age of 8. When he moved to Vienna in 1792 he was helped by patrons, even though he was arrogant and uncouth in his behaviour towards them. Just as he was beginning to achieve recognition as a composer he began to go deaf, but in spite of this tragedy he continued to compose some of his greatest works, many of which he never heard performed.

Helen Keller

Helen Keller was born in Alabama, U.S.A. in 1880. When she was a 20-month-old baby, she became very sick with a high fever. The fever lasted a few days; when it passed, Helen was left without her sight or hearing. No doctor was able to reverse the tragic effects of her illness. Helen was to live the rest of her life in a dark and soundless world. Her parents weren't able to communicate with her and she was unable to learn from them, so she became a frightened, troublesome, and unhappy child. When she was 7 years old, her parents hired a woman named Anne Sullivan, a special teacher, to help her. After some time, Anne was able to communicate with Helen by using the sense of touch. Anne spelled out words with her fingers pressed into the palm of Helen's hands. It was a great breakthrough for Helen, and one which totally changed her life.

Helen went on to graduate with honours from college. She then dedicated her life to the needs of handicapped people by speaking up for them and by raising money for schools and research. Helen also wrote several books, including *The Story of My Life* and *Midstream—My Later Life*. These inspiring books tell of the struggles and needs of handicapped people as seen through the life of one, Helen Keller.

Douglas Bader

Born in London in 1910, he was commissioned in the Royal Air Force in 1930 but lost both legs in a flying accident in 1931. Fitted with two 'tin legs' he was determined to walk again and when war came in 1939 he succeeded in rejoining the R.A.F. As a Squadron Leader in the Battle of Britain he was recognised as a formidable buccaneer of the air and a great fighter ace who contributed his ideas and his skill to winning the battle. In 1941 he crashed in France and was taken prisoner. Returning after the war he took up the cause of the disabled, showing that by courage and will-power handicaps could be overcome. He was knighted for his services in 1956.

Barry Sheen

A Londoner born in 1950, by the age of six Barry Sheen was riding motor bikes in his father's workshop yard, and by the age of 17 he entered his first race. Within a few years he was National 125 cc Champion, and in 1976 and 1977 he was 500 cc World Champion on a Suzuki and a star of the motor-cycle race-track. Still at the peak of his career, he crashed his new V4 Yamaha shattering both legs and a wrist. It seemed he would never ride again, yet his determination and courage 'to race again and be the best' made the miracle happen and within 67 days he was back on the track. He retired from motor-cycle racing in 1985 but since then has raced cars and trucks as courageously as ever.

Stevie Wonder

Singer/songwriter Stevie Wonder was born Steveland Judkins Morris in Michigan, U.S.A., in 1950. He was blind at birth and his family was poor. However, Stevie never let his blindness stop him from composing and performing music. As a very young boy, he was given a harmonica by his family barber. At the young age of 13 he recorded his first hit song 'Fingertips.' Today, he is a wealthy and famous performer. Stevie Wonder has proven his theory that a handicap is a handicap only if a person lets it be one.

Wilma Rudolph

Wilma Rudolph was born in 1940 in Tennessee (U.S.A.). When she was four years old she became ill with scarlet fever followed by pneumonia. She was so sick that her parents feared for her life. Fortunately the doctors were able to save her, but her illness left her without the use of one leg. It was thought that she could never walk again. Wilma's mother was determined to help her overcome her handicap. Years of treatment, braces, special shoes, and sheer determination paid off. Wilma was able to walk again. When she could walk she began to run. Her running took her to the 1960 Olympics where she became the second American woman in history to win three golds medals in a single Olympics.

Itzhak Perlman

Itzhak Perlman was born in Tel Aviv, Israel in 1945. When he was 4 years old he was infected by polio, a disease which crippled him for life. At an early age Itzhak began to play the violin. He had a great gift for music and refused to let his crippled legs keep him from becoming a performer. At the age of 10 he gave his first concert. A talent scout from the United States saw him play and convinced him to go to the U.S. where he appeared on television. He was a great success and his career took off. Today Itzhak Perlman is a world-renowned concert violinist. He walks on stage with the aid of crutches and struggles into his chair, but he plays the violin with brilliance and beauty.

Who Said What

FAMOUS WORDS OF FAMOUS PEOPLE

LAWRENCE OATES,
English Arctic Explorer.
'I am just going outside and may be some time.'

FRANCOIS VOLTAIRE,
French Philosopher.
'I disapprove of what you say, but I will defend to the death your right to say it.'

LORD NELSON,
English Admiral at Battle of Trafalgar.
'England expects every man will do his duty.'

LORD GREY OF FALLODON,
British Statesman on August 3, 1914.
'The lamps are going out all over Europe. We shall not see them lit in our lifetime.'

OSCAR WILDE,
Irish Dramatist at New York Custom House.
'I have nothing to declare but my genius.'

SAM GOLDWYN, *U.S. Film Producer.*	**'A verbal contract isn't worth the paper it's written on.'**
WINSTON CHURCHILL, *British Prime Minister.*	**'Never in the field of human conflict was so much owed by so many to so few.' 'The English never draw a line without blurring it.'**
HAROLD MACMILLAN, *British Prime Minister.*	**'You've never had it so good.'**
AESOP, *Greek fable writer.*	**'Do not count your chickens before they are hatched.'**
WILLIAM SHAKESPEARE, *English playwright.*	**'Sink or swim.'**
BENJAMIN FRANKLIN, *U.S. statesman.*	**'A penny saved is a penny earned.' 'Nothing is certain but death and taxes.'**
ALEXANDER POPE, *English poet.*	**'A little learning is a dangerous thing.'**
ABRAHAM LINCOLN, *U.S. president.*	**'You can't fool all of the people all the time.'**
FRANKLIN D. ROOSEVELT, *U.S. president.*	**'The only thing we have to fear is fear itself.'**
ANNE FRANK, *German Jewish girl; victim of the Nazis.*	**'In spite of everything I still believe that people are really good at heart.'**
JOHN F. KENNEDY, *U.S. president.*	**'Ask not what your country can do for you; ask what you can do for your country.'**
NEIL A. ARMSTRONG, *U.S. astronaut.*	**'That's one small step for man, one great leap for mankind.'**
P.T. BARNUM, *American showman.*	**'There's a sucker born every minute.'**
ALAN BENNETT, *British playwright.*	**'Life is rather like a tin of sardines – we're all of us looking for the key.'**
GEORGE ORWELL, *British author.*	**'All animals are equal. But some animals are more equal than others.'**

Famous People: Real and Legendary

REAL PEOPLE

ANNIE OAKLEY—A renowned sharpshooter with a rifle and shotgun, she travelled with Buffalo Bill's Wild West Show for 17 years. She was born Phoebe Anne Oakley Mozee in Ohio in 1860 and died in 1926.

BOADICCA—A British warrior queen in the 1st century A.D. She led her tribe in war against the Romans, but her army was finally defeated in a battle somewhere between London and Colchester, so she took poison and died.

CAPTAIN KIDD—William Kidd was born in Scotland in 1645. As a seaman he was hired to protect ships from piracy. However, he became a pirate. He was convicted of piracy and hanged in London in 1701.

CLEOPATRA—A true Egyptian queen, she was born in 69 B.C. and died in 30 B.C. For 30 years she fought with her brother, Ptolemy, for control of Egypt. Finally she allied herself with Roman emperor, Julius Caesar, who defeated her brother in war. She married Mark Antony, Julius Caesar's successor.

DAVY CROCKETT—A great hero of frontier America, Crockett was born in Tennessee in 1786. He fought in Indian wars, served in the U.S. House of Representatives, and died in 1836 defending the Alamo in Texas.

JESSE JAMES—This notorious U.S. outlaw was famous for his train and bank robberies. He was born in Missouri in 1847, and was killed by one of his own gang members in 1882.

POCAHONTAS—She was born in Virginia in 1595 and died in 1617. Pocahontas saved the life of the English settler, Captain John Smith, and helped to keep relationships friendly between the English settlers of Jamestown, Virginia and the Indians. She married John Rolfe, a Jamestown settler.

SITTING BULL—A Sioux Indian from South Dakota, he was a leader in the Indian resistance that led to the famous Battle of Little Bighorn. Also a famous medicine man, he later toured with Buffalo Bill's Wild West Show. He was born in 1831 and died in 1890.

TOM THUMB—Charles Sherwood Stratton was an American midget who became known by his circus name, General Tom Thumb. When fully grown, he was 2 feet tall and weighed 70 pounds. He joined P.T. Barnum's travelling show and became a world-famous show business personality. Tom Thumb was born in Connecticut in 1838. He died in 1883 at the age of 45.

LEGENDARY PEOPLE

DRACULA—The story of Dracula, the Transylvanian count who was a vampire, was written by the British novelist, Bram Stoker (1847–1912).

FU MANCHU—The Chinese criminal genius was created by Englishman Sax Rohmer (1883–1959) who wrote 13 books about Fu Manchu.

KING ARTHUR—Mention of Arthur as the leader of the Britons first occurs in an imaginary history written A.D. 900. It appears that he was based on Celtic legends and Greek myths. Sir Thomas Malory's *Le Morte D'Arthur*, written about 1450, is a partial translation from the French and inspired Tennyson's romantic *Idylls of the Kings*, published in 1859.

ROBIN HOOD—An English folk hero of the Middle Ages, he was said to live in Sherwood Forest where he robbed from the rich and shared his spoils with the poor. His story has been told in books and movies. Although many have tried, no one has yet been able to prove that he really existed.

ROBINSON CRUSOE—He was created by the English novelist Daniel Defoe. The story of Robinson Crusoe was based on the real-life experience of a Scottish sailor named Alexander Selkirk, who lived alone on the island of Juan Fernandez in the Pacific Ocean for four years before he was eventually rescued.

ROMEO AND JULIET—These two famous lovers of Verona, Italy married against the wishes of their families. After their deaths, the feuding families made a peace. The characters were created by Matteo Bandello, a 16th-century Italian writer. Their story was made famous by William Shakespeare, who wrote a play about them.

SHERLOCK HOLMES—This famous English private detective was a character who first appeared in Arthur Conan Doyle's, *A Study in Scarlet*. In over 50 stories, published from 1892–1915, Holmes is portrayed as an exceptional detective who wears a dressing gown, smokes a pipe, and plays a violin.

TARZAN—This famous man of the jungle was a creation of Chicagoan Edgar Rice Burroughs. Burroughs was born in 1875 and wrote 23 Tarzan books before his death in 1950.

THE THREE MUSKETEERS—These courageous young men of 17th-century France, who worked for King Louis XII, were characters created by French author, Alexander Dumas. Dumas wrote this popular adventure story in 1844.

UNCLE SAM—The U.S. government is often symbolized by a tall, white-haired bearded man, known as Uncle Sam. Sam Wilson supplied meat to the U.S. Army in the War of 1812. He stamped the barrels of meat 'U.S.' and people said it stood for 'Uncle Sam.' This nickname was an unfriendly term used by people who were against the war. In 1816, the nickname appeared in a book called *The Adventures of Uncle Sam*. The costume of stars and stripes was a creation of an 1830 cartoon.

Famous Name Changes

REAL NAMES OF TEN FAMOUS PEOPLE

Billy the Kid	William H. Bonney (1859–1881), U.S. outlaw.
Bloody Mary	Mary I (1516–1558), Queen of England.
Buffalo Bill	Colonel William F. Cody (1846–1917), U.S. buffalo hunter, Indian scout, and showman.

PEOPLE

Calamity Jane	Martha Jane Burke (1852–1903), U.S. fr[illegible] woman.
Confucius	K'ung Fu-tzu (551 B.C.–479 B.C.), Chinese philosopher.
Diamond Jim Brady	James Buchanan Brady (1856–1917), U.S. financier.
Adolf Hitler	Adolf Schicklgruber (1889–1945), German dictator.

REAL NAMES OF POPULAR CELEBRITIES

Woody Allen	Allen Steward Konigsberg
Fred Astaire	Fred Austerlitz
Cilla Black	Priscilla White
David Bowie	David Jones
Richard Burton	Richard Jenkins
Michael Caine	Maurice Micklewhite
Sean Connery	Thomas Conner
Elvis Costello	Declan Aloysius Macmanus
Sandra Dee	Alexandra Zuck
Diana Dors	Diana Fluck
Bob Dylan	Robert Zimmerman
David Essex	David Cook
Greta Garbo	Greta Gustafson
Cary Grant	Archibald Leach
Elton John	Reginald Dwight
Boris Karloff	William Pratt
Marilyn Monroe	Norma Jean Baker
Cliff Richard	Harry Webb
John Wayne	Marion Morrison

Stevie Wonder	Stephen Judkins
Mark Twain	Samuel Clemens (1835–1910), U.S. writer.
Muhammed Ali	Cassius Marcellus Clay (1942–), U.S. boxer.
Lord Haw-Haw	William Joyce (1906–46), war-time broadcaster from Germany, hung for treason.

Prime Ministers of Great Britain

The First Prime Minister	Sir Robert Walpole from 1721.
Prime Ministers who died while in office	Henry Pelham in 1754. George Canning in 1827. Viscount Palmerston in 1865.
The Prime Minister who was assassinated	Spencer Perceval was shot in the lobby of the House of Commons in 1812.
The Prime Minister who, early in his career, was imprisoned in the Tower of London	Robert Walpole who was accused of corruption in 1712.
Prime Ministers who fought duels	George Canning with Lord Castlereagh in 1809 Duke of Wellington with Lord Winchelsea in 1829
Prime Ministers who were brothers	Henry Pelham Duke of Newcastle
Prime Ministers who were father and son	Earl of Chatham William Pitt the Younger
The Prime Minister who first introduced Income Tax	William Pitt in 1799
The Prime Minister who served the shortest term	George Canning who died in 1827, 100 days after taking office.
The longest serving Prime Minister	Sir Robert Walpole (1721 – 42)
The Youngest Prime Minister to take office	William Pitt at the age of 24 in 1783

The oldest Prime Minister to take office	William Gladstone began his fourth term in 1892 at the age of 83
First Woman Prime Minister	Margaret Thatcher in 1979

Presidents of the United States

First President	George Washington (1789–1797)
Presidents who died in Office	William Henry Harrison in 1841 Zachary Taylor in 1850 Warren G. Harding in 1923 Franklin D. Roosevelt in 1945
Presidents who were assassinated	Abraham Lincoln in 1865 James A. Garfield in 1881 William McKinley in 1901 John F. Kennedy in 1963
Shortest term of office	William H. Harrison died after serving only 32 days as President in 1841
Longest lived	John Adams became President in 1779 at the age of 61 and served 4 years, but lived for a further 25 years after his term
Longest term of office	Franklin D. Roosevelt was elected 4 times. He served for 12 years and 39 days
Tallest	Abraham Lincoln was 6 feet 4 inches tall
Shortest	James Madison was the shortest as he was only 5 feet 4 inches tall
Youngest	Theodore Roosevelt was 42 years and 10 months old when he took office following the assassination of President McKinley
Youngest elected President	John F. Kennedy was 43 years and 236 days when he took the oath of office
Oldest elected President	Ronald Reagan was 69 when he took office, and was re-elected at the age of 74

Religions of the World

Information about eight major world religions are to be found in this chapter. You can find out for yourself how they teach men to be good—each one in its own way.

> 'Every religion is good that teaches man to be good.'
> —THOMAS PAINE,
> *American Statesman*

BUDDHISM

• Founded about 500 B.C. by Prince Siddhartha Gautama (the Buddha) near Benares, India.
• Practised mainly in Sri Lanka, Thailand and Japan.
• The symbol of this religion is an eight-spoked wheel. Each spoke represents a step toward peace of mind and an end to suffering. It is called the 'eightfold path.'

Step 1—Right knowledge
Step 2—Right intention
Step 3—Right speech
Step 4—Right conduct
Step 5—Right means of livelihood
Step 6—Right effort
Step 7—Right mindfulness
Step 8—Right concentration

• The sacred book is the *Tripitaka*, a collection of Buddha's teachings.
• There are no gods but Buddhists worship images of Buddha.
• Followers practise yoga and meditation.
• Buddhists believe that people are born and reborn over and over again. When they achieve enlightenment they are finally freed from all desire and the cycle of rebirth. They have then reached Nirvana.

CHRISTIANITY

• Founded by followers of Jesus Christ after 4 A.D.
• The most popular religion in the world. Over one-fifth of world's population follow one of its sects.
• Practised mainly in Europe, America, Australasia and Southern Africa.
• The holy book is the *Bible* which consists of the Old Testament and New Testament (Christ's life and teachings).

- There are hundreds of Christian groups called denominations. Their beliefs and practices vary.
- Christians believe in one God and in Jesus Christ as the son of God. God redeemed the sins of humans when Jesus Christ was crucified and died on the cross. He then ascended to heaven as the son of God.
- In Christian teaching the soul lives after the body dies. The soul goes to heaven to live with God or to hell for eternal damnation.

CONFUCIANISM

- Founded in China in the 6th century B.C. by Confucius (K'ung Fu-tzu).
- Practised mainly in China, and Taiwan.
- Believe in heaven, ancestor worship, and many gods.
- Sacred books, the *Analects* (*Lun Yu*) and the *Wu Ching* (fire classics), ancient Chinese writings.
- Believe in afterlife with ancestors in heaven.
- No clergy.

HINDUISM

- Began, c. 1500 B.C.; the founder is unknown.
- Practised mainly in India.
- Hindus are born to their religion. There are no converts.
- The sacred text is the *Veda*, a collection of myths, epic stories, and rituals.
- There are hundreds of gods and goddesses, enough so that each family has a favourite to honour.
- Followers believe in a cycle of birth and rebirth. Each life is determined by past deeds called Karma. (The concept of Karma is also shared by Buddhists.)

ISLAM

- Founded in 622 A.D. by Mohammed, the Prophet, in Medina, Arabia.
- Followers of Islam are called Moslems.
- Practised from West Africa to Indonesia.
- The holy book is the *Koran*, which contains the words of God (Allah) as told by Mohammed.
- Islam means submission to Allah. All the earth belongs to Allah which is why Moslems pray on the ground.
- Followers believe their bodies die but their souls live forever in heaven or hell.
- The five pillars of faith of Islam are:
    1. Belief in Allah.
    2. Prayer 5 times a day.
    3. Donating to charity.
    4. Fasting from sunrise to sunset during the month of Ramadan.
    5. Making a pilgrimage to Mecca at least once in a lifetime.

JUDAISM

- Founded by Abraham more than 5,000 years ago.
- The major areas of practise are Israel, the U.S., and the U.S.S.R.
- The holy book is the *Torah* (the first five books of the Old Testament).
- Followers believe in one God, Jehovah, who is the creator and ruler of the Universe.
- Jews believe their souls will live forever.

SHINTO

- Founded in antiquity but influenced by Confucianism and Buddhism.
- Practised in Japan.
- *Shin–to* means the 'way of the Spirit.'
- Followers believe that the Sun-goddess, Amateras, was the original Mother of the line of Millados (Emperors), so the Emperor is a divine being. Emperor Hirohito officially renounced the idea of divinity on December 31, 1945.
- Followers believe that all human beings are the offspring of nature, so whatever they think or do must be natural and therefore right.
- Shinto worship consists of keeping on good terms with the numerous *Kami* or gods.

TAOISM

- Founded in 600 B.C. by Lao-Tze in China.
- Practised mainly in China.
- The sacred book is the *Tao-te-Ching*.
- Tao means a way or a road.
- Followers believe in the yin and yang of the Universe. *Yin* represents the earth; *yang* represents heaven. The balance of yin and yang give order to the world. People are encouraged to work in harmony with nature.

Sports

'The important thing in the Olympic Games is not to win, but to take part; the important thing in life is not the triumph but the struggle; the essential thing is not having conquered but to have fought well.'

—BARON PIERRE DE COUBERTIN,
father of the modern Olympic Games

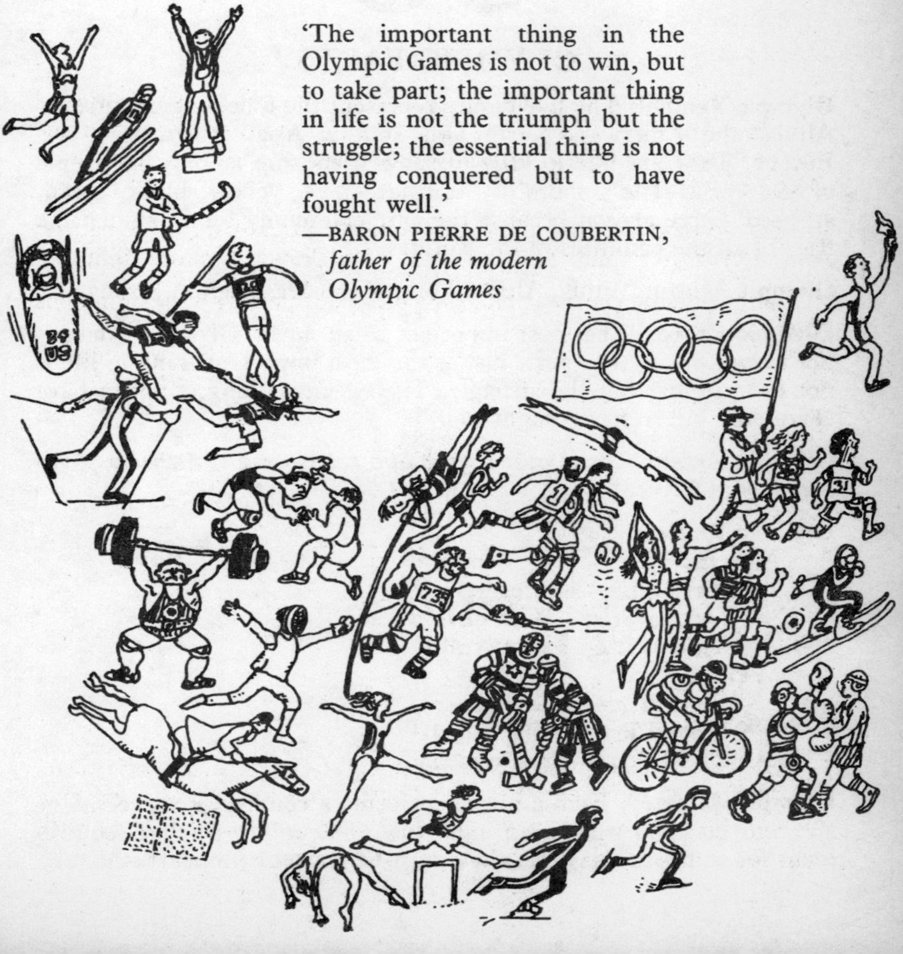

Olympic Sports

The Olympic Games are the ultimate competition for the amateur athlete. They are held every four years in various countries throughout the world.

OLYMPIC FACTS

Olympic Symbol: The five circles represent the following continents: Africa, the Americas (North and South), Asia, Australasia, and Europe. They are interlocking to show friendship among the people of the world. The colours of the rings—blue, yellow, black, green, and red—were chosen because they are commonly found among the flags of all the countries of the world.

Olympic Motto: 'Citius, Altius, Fortius' (Faster, Higher, Stronger).

Olympic Creed: 'The most important thing in the Olympic games is not to win but to take part, just as the most important thing in life is not the triumph but the struggle. The essential thing is not to have conquered but to have fought well.'

Olympic Hymn: 'The Hymn Olympique' (composed in 1896 by Spyro Samaras of Greece).

Olympic Prizes:

Ancient
—First Prize—Laurel wreath
Second Prize—Wild olive wreath
Third Prize—Palm wreath

Modern
—First Prize—Gold medal
Second Prize—Silver medal
Third Prize—Bronze medal

Olympic Athletes: Each athlete represents a country; however he or she competes and wins as an individual. The only restrictive requirement for competitors is that they must be amateur (unpaid) athletes.

Countries Represented in the Olympics: Ancient Olympics—one country (Greece).

First Modern Olympics—Thirteen countries.

Present-Day Olympics—more than 120 countries.

THE OFFICIAL OLYMPIC SPORTS

Summer Sports

Archery—Men, Women
Basketball—Men, Women
Boxing—Men
Canoeing—Men, Women
Cycling—Men, Women
Equestrian Games (horse riding)—Men, Women
Fencing—Men, Women
Field Hockey—Men, Women
Gymnastics—Men, Women
Judo—Men
Modern Pentathlon (cross-country running, fencing, riding, shooting, and swimming)—Men
Rowing—Men, Women
Shooting—Men, Women
Soccer—Men
Swimming and Diving—Men, Women
Track and Field—Men, Women
Team Handball—Men, Women
Volleyball—Men, Women
Water Polo—Men
Weightlifting—Men
Wrestling (freestyle and Greco-Roman)—Men
Yachting—Men, Women

Winter Sports

Biathlon (skiing and shooting)—Men
Bobsledding—Men
Figure Skating—Men, Women
Ice Dancing—Men, Women
Ice Hockey—Men
Luge (sledding)—Men, Women
Skiing (Nordic and Alpine)—Men, Women
Speed Skating—Men, Women

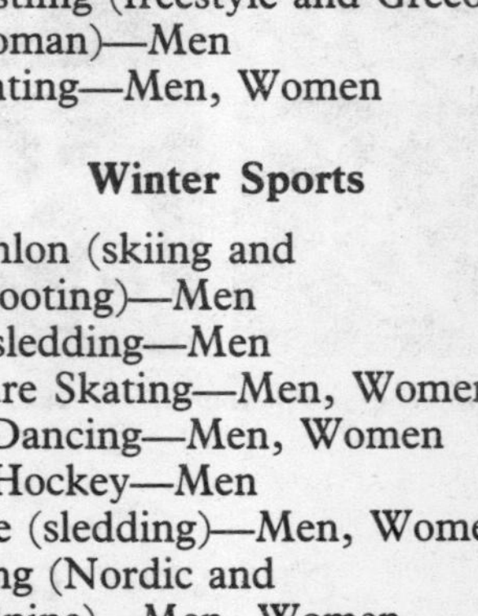

OLYMPIC SYMBOLS

Olympic sports pictograms © 1981, Los Angeles Olympic Organizing Committee

OLYMPIC GAMES MILESTONES

B.C.

776 The first recorded Olympics were held in Olympia, Greece. There was only one sporting event. It was a race of 200 yards. These Olympics were held for 1,168 years—a total of 242 Olympiads.

A.D.

394 The ancient Olympic Games were banned by the Romans.

1896 The first modern Olympic Games were held in Athens, Greece. Baron Pierre de Coubertin, a Frenchman, founded the Games to foster sportsmanship among athletes and to create goodwill among people of all countries.

1900 Women were allowed to compete in the Games. Six women participated in lawn tennis.

1920 The Flight of Doves was officially introduced to the opening ceremony of the Olympics.

1924 The winter Games were held for the first time. They were contested at Chamonix, France.

1928 The Olympic torch was lit for the first time at the Amsterdam Games.

1936 These were the first televised games and included the first lighted torch relay—from Olympia, Greece, to Berlin, the site of the Games.

1968 Athletes who participated in women's events were required to take a femininity control exam, to be sure they were women.

1984 The summer Games became the most televised in history when ABC (the American Broadcasting Company) bought the rights to show 200 hours of sports over a 2-week period.

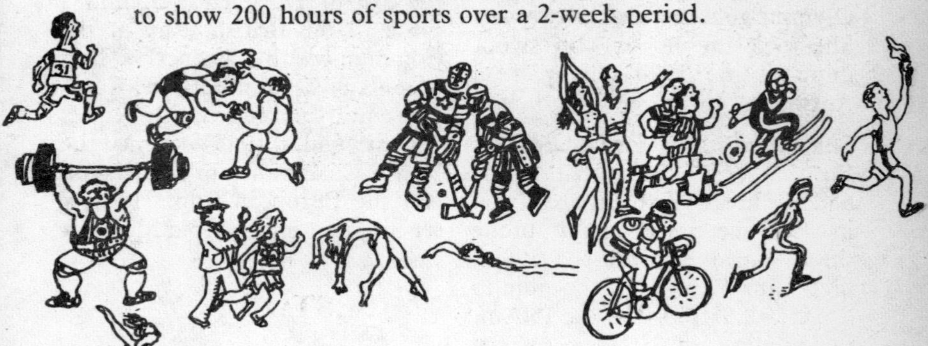

Memorable Olympic Athletes

Vasili Alexeyev, U.S.S.R. This 345–lb. superweight set a world record when he lifted 562 lbs. to become the world's strongest man. He won gold medals in the 1972 and 1976 summer Games.

Robert Beamon, U.S.A. His 29–foot, 2½-inch long jump at the 1968 Olympics was hailed as one of the greatest athletic achievements. It was 21¾ inches longer than the world record.

Joan Benoit, U.S.A. She won the first Olympic women's marathon at the 1984 Los Angeles Summer Games.

Abebe Bikila, Ethiopia. He was the first to win the marathon twice, in 1960 and 1964. He was also the first gold medallist from black Africa. In 1960, he ran the entire 26.7-mile marathon barefoot.

Francine Blankers, Holland. This 30-year-old mother was known as 'Marvellous Mama' at the 1948 London Olympics where she won four gold medals in track and field events.

Ethelda Bleibtrey, U.S.A. She was the first woman to win three Olympic gold medals in any sport. She took the honours in swimming at the 1920 Olympics in Antwerp.

Sebastian Coe, Great Britain. Born in West London in 1956, he had made so much progress that in 1979 he sensationally broke three World Records–the 800m. in 1 min. 42.33 sec.; the mile in 3 min. 48.95 sec; and the 1500m. in 3 min. 32.03 sec. At the Moscow Olympics, where he was the favourite to win, he lost to Steve Ovett. Yet he gained the Gold Medal in the 1500m, a feat he repeated in the 1984 Games when he beat Steve Cram into second place—three superb athletes who made these track events a particularly British occasion.

Nadia Comaneci, Romania. At the age of 14 she became the first gymnast to score a perfect 10. Altogether she won three gold medals, a silver, and a bronze at the Montreal Olympics in 1976. In Moscow, 1980 she won two more gold medals.

James B. Connolly, U.S.A. He was the first person to win a gold medal in the modern Olympic Games. He won the gold in the triple jump in Athens, Greece in 1896.

Steve Cram, Great Britain. Born on Tyneside in 1960 he achieved his first great success in athletics with a remarkable record time of 3 min. 57.4 sec. for the mile at the age of 17. That won him a place in the British team at the Commonwealth Games. Two years later he won both the European and Commonwealth Games 1500m., and in 1983 he gained the World Championship at Helsinki and the European Cup. He now set his heart on the Gold Medal at

the 1984 Olympics but after winning his heat and the semi-finals he was beaten into second place by his old rival Sebastian Coe. In July 1985 at Nice he ran a world record 1500m. when he and Said Aouita became the first to run the distance in less than 3½ minutes. In the same month he set two more world records at the mile and 2000m. A truly remarkable track athlete.

Mildred 'Babe' Didrikson, U.S.A. She was one of the first females to be an Olympic star. An all-around athlete, she won a gold medal in the javelin and the hurdles, and a silver medal in the high jump at the 1932 Olympics in Los Angeles.

Eddie Eagan, U.S.A. He is the only athlete to win gold medals in both the winter and summer Games. He won the first in boxing at the 1920 summer Games and a second in bobsledding at the 1932 winter Games.

Kornelia Ender, East Germany. She is one of the greatest female swimmers of all time. She won 4 gold medals at the 1976 Montreal Games.

Ray Ewry, U.S.A. Known as 'the rubber man,' this track and field star won an all-time record string of ten consecutive Olympic championships from 1900–1908. His wins were in the standing high jump, standing long jump, and standing triple jump.

Dick Fosbury, U.S.A. He was the first Olympic high jumper to go over the pole head first, landing on his back. This style known as the 'Fosbury Flop' earned him a gold medal in Mexico in 1968 and set a new trend in high jumping.

Shane Gould, Australia. This great swimmer won three gold medals, a silver, and bronze in the 1972 Olympics. She also broke world records in 3 swimming events in the same Olympics.

Eric Heiden, U.S.A. Considered the greatest men's speed skater in history, he won five gold medals in the 1980 Winter Olympics in Lake Placid. He was the only athlete to win five individual golds in the history of the Winter Olympics.

Sonja Henie, Norway. A world champion figure skater, she first competed at the age of 10 in 1924. She did not win that year but went on to win gold medals in the 1928, 1932, and 1936 Olympics.

Ivan Johansson, Sweden. The top Swedish wrestler, he won three gold medals in wrestling, two in 1932 and one in 1936.

Olga Korbut, U.S.S.R. This great Olympic gymnast won three gold medals at the age of 17 in 1972. At the following Olympics in 1976 she won another gold and two silver medals. She is famous for inspiring many youngsters to take up the sport of gymnastics.

Alvin Kraenzlein, U.S.A. He won four individual championships in 1900. He won the 60-metre sprint, 110-metre high hurdles, 200-metre low hurdles, and the long jump.

Carl Lewis, U.S.A. He won four gold medals for track and field events at the 1984 Summer Games in Los Angeles. He excelled in the long jump, the 100 metre, 200 metre and the relay.

Bob Mathias, U.S.A. At the age of 17 he upset the field in the 1948 decathlon by winning the gold. He won again in 1952 and became the first athlete to win the Olympic decathlon twice.

Paavo Nurmi, Finland. The 'Flying Finn' as he was called, set 22 world records, and won nine golds and three silvers in middle and long distance races. He participated in the 1924 and 1928 Winter Olympics.

Alfred Oerter, U.S.A. His record wins as a discus thrower have never been matched. From 1956 to 1968 he won 4 consecutive gold medals.

James 'Jesse' Owens, U.S.A. The hero of the 1936 Berlin, Olympic Games, Owens won four gold medals in track and field. He is also remembered for Adolf Hitler's refusal to shake hands with him because he was black.

Tamara Press, U.S.S.R. She is one of the top field-event women in the world. Weighing in at 220 pounds, she won the shot put title in 1960 and 1964. In 1964 she also won the discus.

Peter Snell, New Zealand. He is remembered as the only athlete to win three Olympic gold medals in mid-distance races. He won two in 1960 and one in 1964.

Mark Spitz, U.S.A. He dominated the 1972 Olympics in swimming. He entered seven events and won seven gold medals in

individual and team events. No athlete before him had ever won as many as seven golds in one Olympiad.

Oscar Swahn, Sweden. At age 72 he was the oldest person to win an Olympic medal. A legendary target shooter, he won three gold, one silver and two bronze medals in the 1908 and 1912 Olympics.

Daley Thompson, Great Britain. Born in London, Daley is one of the great characters of athletics—wildly enthusiastic, good humoured and highly ambitious. In 1978 he won a Commonwealth gold medal in the decathlon events; in 1980 he won the Olympic Decathlon; in 1982 he was the first man to hold the European, Commonwealth and Olympic titles, and in 1984 he was awarded the Olympic gold–a remarkable record for such a testing series of events.

James 'Jim' Thorpe, U.S.A. This native American was one of the greatest athletes of all time and the only one to win both the decathlon and pentathlon (1912). In 1913 his medals were taken away because it was learned that he played semi-professional baseball in 1909 (all Olympic participants must be amateurs). In 1982, twenty years after his death, Thorpe's medals were returned to his family. His wins were once again recorded in Olympic history.

Johnny Weissmuller, U.S.A. Considered the greatest swimmer of the first half of the 20th century, he won five gold medals in the 1924 and 1928 Olympics. Later, he became famous as 'Tarzan' in the movies.

MODERN OLYMPIC GAMES WHERE THEY WERE HELD

I 1896 Athens, Greece	13 countries took part, but most of the 311 competitors were Greeks.
II 1900 Paris, France	22 countries took part and the events were spread over a 5-month period.
III 1904 St. Louis, USA	13 countries represented but majority of the competitors were Americans who won most of the medals.

	1906 Athens, Greece	Interim games held to celebrate the 10th anniversary.
IV	1908 London, England	Over 2,000 competitors from 22 countries competed over a period of 6 months. The White City Stadium was built for the purpose.
V	1912 Stockholm, Sweden	The number of sports were reduced and the games confined to 11 weeks.
VI	1916	Not held due to the war.
VII	1920 Antwerp, Belgium	The Olympic oath and the Olympic flag were first introduced.
VIII	1924 Paris, France	Johnny Weismuller, later made famous in the 'Tarzan' films, won three gold medals for swimming.
IX	1928 Amsterdam, Netherlands	The start was marked by the release of hundreds of pigeons and the burning of the Olympic flame throughout the games.
X	1932 Los Angeles, USA	An Olympic Village was provided for the first time and a photo-finish camera used for track events.
XI	1936 Berlin, Germany	Opened by Adolf Hitler who used it to display the efficiency of the Nazi regime. For the first time a flaming torch was carried from Athens to start the games.
XII	1940	Not held due to the war.
XIII	1944	Not held due to the war
XIV	1948 London, England	An austerity Olympics, as England was still trying to recover from the effects of the war.

XV	1952 Helsinki, Finland	69 countries and nearly 5,000 competitors took part.
XVI	1956 Melbourne, Australia	The equestrian events were held in Stockholm. For the first time the Soviet Union won more medals than the USA, and Australia was third.
XVII	1960 Rome, Italy	An Ethiopian, Abebe Bikila, won the marathon running barefoot.
XVIII	1964 Tokyo, Japan	Bikila won the marathon for the second time–the first man to win the race twice.
XIX	1968 Mexico City, Mexico	Over a hundred (112) countries competed for the first time.
XX	1972 Munich, Germany	Television came into its own—over 1,000 million viewers watched the Opening Ceremony.
XXI	1976 Montreal, Canada	Boycotted by 20 Third World Countries protesting at the inclusion of New Zealand which had allowed a Rugby team to visit South Africa. The Olympic torch went out when it was doused by a cloudburst.
XXII	1980 Moscow, USSR	Many countries, including the United States, West Germany and Japan, boycotted the games as a protest at Russia's invasion of Afghanistan.
XXIII	1984 Los Angeles, USA	Russia and 14 other countries in the Communist Bloc boycotted the games, thereby reducing much of its competitive interest.
XXIV	1988 Seoul, South Korea and North Korea	

Transportation

In this chapter you can read about nearly every vehicle made to move people around this world and out of this world. Here you'll find the first, the fastest, and other interesting facts about transportation.

Transportation on Water

FIRSTS ON WATER

- The ancient Sumerians built the first known oar-powered ships to carry them on the Tigris and Euphrates rivers in 3500 B.C.
- The first submarine was a leather-covered boat built in 1620 by a Dutchman, Cornelis Drebbel.
- The American inventor, John Fitch, was the first to demonstrate the steamboat as a means of transportation. In 1787 he launched it on the Delaware River. Four years later he patented his invention.
- In 1906, Enrico Forlanini of Italy invented the hydrofoil, a vessel which moved over water. Three sets of stilts or foils lift it above the water to reduce drag. Commercial use of the hydrofoil began in the 1930s.
- The hovercraft, which moves over the surface of the water supported by a cushion of air, was invented in 1955 by Sir Christopher Cockerell of Great Britain. Hovercrafts are also used to travel over swamps, snow, and sand.

• The first nuclear-powered vessel was launched in 1954 by the U.S. This submarine, the USS *Nautilus*, needed no air for its motors and could make long underwater journeys without refuelling. It was also the first sea vessel to reach the North Pole. Able to dive 750 feet, it travelled under ice to reach the northernmost point on the Earth in 1958.

FAMOUS SEACRAFT

MARY CELESTE

The American brigantine left New York on November 7, 1872 with ten people on board. On December 5 she was sighted drifting near the Azores with no sign of life aboard. A half-eaten meal, clothes and even pipes were left abandoned and no survivor was ever found. The ghostly discovery of the *Mary Celeste* is still one of the great mysteries of the sea.

HMS MARY ROSE

Henry VIII's flagship, originally built in 1509–11, set sail from Spithead on July 19 1545 to engage the French fleet threatening invasion. Heavily laden with a crew and soldiers numbering some 700 or more, and well stocked with ammunition, it heeled over within sight of land. In the 1960s the wreck was discovered, and in 1982 it was recovered from the seabed. Now the hull of the great ship, and thousands of articles salvaged from it, can be seen at Portsmouth.

H.M.S. BOUNTY

This ship was the scene of one of the most famous mutinies in history. In 1701 the *Bounty* sailed under the English flag to the South Pacific. Its mission was to gather breadfruit trees to transplant to English colonies in the West Indies. First mate, Fletcher Christian, led a mutiny against Captain William Bligh. Bligh was cast adrift with 18 others in an open boat. They sailed nearly 4,000 miles in the small boat to reach safety in the East Indies. Some of the mutineers, including Christian, sailed to Pitcairn Island in the South Pacific. They founded a colony where their descendants continue to live.

CLERMONT

Dubbed 'Fulton's Folly' by non-believers, this boat achieved fame as the first commercially successful steamboat. In 1807, Robert Fulton navigated it 240 miles on the Hudson river from New York City to Albany and back. The entire journey took 63 hours.

CONNECTICUT TURTLE
This was the first submarine used in warfare. Built by 34-year-old American, David Bushnell, it was used by the Americans against British ships in 1776.

U.S.S. CONSTITUTION
This American warship was used in the War of 1812. It was nicknamed 'Old Ironsides' because cannonballs seemed to bounce right off her. After 100 years of service it was retired. It can still be visited at dock in Boston, U.S.A.

GOLDEN HIND
The flagship of the renowned British seaman Sir Francis Drake, the *Golden Hind* was the only one of his five ships to complete a voyage around the world (1577–1580). Drake was knighted on board and the ship was put on display in Deptford dockyard in England where it remained for over a century.

S.S. GREAT BRITAIN
Designed by Isambard Kingdom Brunel, the *Great Britain* was the 322-foot-long ship—the largest in the world when launched in 1840. It was the first transatlantic screw-driven iron ship, and it was in service until 1886. She can now be visited at Bristol, where she was built.

KON-TIKI
In 1947 Norwegian Thor Heyerdahl built a replica of the balsam rafts used by the natives of the South Pacific. He travelled in this raft from South America to the Polynesian Islands by drifting 4,300 miles with the wind. Heyerdahl made the journey to prove his theory that the people of Polynesia originated in South America.

LUSITANIA

A British passenger ship, the *Lusitania* was torpedoed by German submarines on May 7, 1915. The boat sank in 20 minutes, and 1,195 lives were lost; among them 128 Americans. The U.S. was not involved in World War 1 at the time and protested at the sinking to the German government.

MAYFLOWER

In 1620 this small ship (90 feet long) set sail with 130 passengers and crew from Southampton, England. The ship was heading across the Atlantic to Virginia in America. Tossed about by a storm, it was thrown off course, and landed in Plymouth, Massachusetts on December 21. One hundred and two passengers, who were pilgrims seeking religious freedom in America, disembarked. The *Mayflower* returned to England the following April.

NINA, PINTA, AND SANTA MARIA

Christopher Columbus sailed from Spain on August 3, 1492 on the flagship the *Santa Maria*. The three ships of the expedition carried a total of 88 men. They sighted San Salvador in the New World on October 12, 1492. On Christmas day of the same year, the *Santa Maria* was wrecked off the shore of Haiti. The wood from the ship was used to build a fort on the island. Columbus and his men returned to Spain on the *Nina* and the *Pinta*.

QUEEN ELIZABETH

The largest passenger liner ever built, the *Queen Elizabeth* was launched in 1938. This British ship was built as a luxury liner for 2,000 passengers. During World War II it was used to transport entire army divisions.

TITANIC
This British transatlantic passenger ship was thought to be extremely safe and unsinkable. In 1912, on its maiden voyage to New York, it struck an iceberg. The ship sank and 1,589 passengers and crew drowned. Although the ship's capacity was more than 2,000, there were lifeboats for only 1,178 people. After this tragedy, safety drills and sufficient lifeboats became mandatory on all ships.

TRITON
In 1960 this submarine became the first to circumnavigate the world. It covered 36,014 miles in 76 days.

HMS VICTORY
The Royal Navy's most famous ship was launched in 1765. A three-decker, she carried a formidable array of guns. She wore the flags of many of Britain's most distinguished admirals including Howe, Hood and St. Vincent and was Nelson's flagship at the Battle of Trafalgar on 21 October 1805 which ended Napoleon's hopes of invading England and Nelson's life. HMS *Victory* was withdrawn from active service in 1812 and can now be visited at Portsmouth.

HMS WARRIOR
First iron-clad warship; HMS *Warrior* was launched in 1860 and commissioned the following year. The iron hull was armoured with 4½ inches of wrought-iron backed by 18 inches of teak, and was the largest, fastest, best protected and most formidable warship in the world. Rescued from an ignominous life as a floating jetty at Pembroke Dock, she has now been refitted, complete with masts and furled sails, 34 muzzle and breech loading guns and a massive replica of the original engine. She will be moved to Portsmouth and open to visitors in Spring/Summer 1987.

Transportation on Land

FIRSTS ON LAND

B.C.

3500 The first wheeled vehicles were drawn by animals and used in Mesopotamia.

1675 The Egyptians used the first horse-drawn chariots for battle.

170 The world's first paved streets, which were passable in all weather, were built by the Romans.

A.D.

44 The Chinese invented the wheel barrow.

1638 The first English stagecoaches began service. Roads and inns were built to accommodate travellers.

1662 The first city bus service was inaugurated in Paris. The horse-drawn buses could accommodate eight people. They were called 'Carrosses à Cinq Sous' because for five sous a passenger could travel any distance on the bus line.

1769 The first self-driven carriage was propelled by steam. It was invented by Nicolas Cugnot of France. It was a three-wheeled vehicle with an 'engine' on the front wheel. The first motor vehicle accident in history took place when Cugnot ran into a wall driving this machine.

1791 The first bicycle was built by the Comte de Sirvac of France. It was a two-wheeled wooden machine with a seat. The rider sat on the seat and 'walked' the bike, as there were no pedals.

1804 The first commercial locomotive was built by Cornishman Richard Trevithick.

1863 First underground railway opened in London.

1869 American George Westinghouse patented a pneumatic (air-filled) brake for trains. It is still the most widely-used train brake.

1869 The first known motorcycle was built in France. It was a pedal bicycle fitted with a small steam engine.

1873 The first cable streetcar in the world was built in San Francisco.

1886 Gottlieb Daimler of Germany built the first four-wheeled, petrol-driven vehicle. The same year, another German, Karl Benz, built a petrol-driven automobile with three wheels.

1888 The pneumatic (air-filled) bicycle tyre was invented by John Dunlop of Belfast, Ireland. By using rubber sheeting and strips of fabric he made a tyre that would cushion his son's bike rides on the cobble-stone streets of Belfast. He was awarded a patent for his invention.

1889 American Nellie Bly gained international acclaim by travelling around the world in 72 days, 6 hours, and 11 minutes. The journalist travelled by train, ship, horse, sampan, and rickshaw to outdo the fictitious Phineas Fogg of the Jules Verne story, *Around the World in 80 Days*.

1897 The first subway line in the U.S. was opened in Boston.

LEGENDARY TRAINS

THE WORLD'S FIRSTS
The Stockton and Darlington Railway was opened in 1825—the first regularly operated steam railway, carrying freight. The first regular passenger service commenced in 1830 between Liverpool and Manchester with the train drawn by George Stephenson's 'Rocket'.

ELECTRIC RAILWAY
The first public electric railway opened in Brighton in 1883.

THE BLUE TRAIN
Considered the most luxurious train in the world, it was built in 1972 to run from Pretoria to Capetown, South Africa. It accommodates 108 passengers in its 16 coaches. Everyone has a private room. It has been called a five-star hotel on wheels.

ORIENT EXPRESS
This is the most famous train in history. It began service in 1883 taking passengers from Paris to Constantinople (now Istanbul). Spies frequented this 'train of Kings' and thieves stole from its rich passen-

gers. It was the setting for three famous novels; *From Russia With Love*, *Murder on the Orient Express*, and *Stamboul Train*.

PIONEER
In 1853 this Chicago train was equipped with the first practical sleeping car. George Pullman, a New York cabinetmaker, devised the convertible berths that pulled down for sleeping. These cars became known as Pullman cars.

SHINKANSEN
Also known as the Bullet trains, these Japanese trains were designed in 1964 to provide the fastest passenger service in the world. The trains run from Tokyo to Osaka at an average speed of 103 mph. They can reach a top speed of 159 mph. The recently-built French Electric trains (TGVs) can now match the speed of 'The Bullets.'

TRANS-SIBERIAN RAILROAD
This Russian railway is the longest railway line in the world. It has 5,799 miles of track that extend from Moscow to Vladivostok. There are 97 stops and the complete journey takes 7 days and 2 hours to complete.

NOTABLE AUTOMOBILES

CITROEN (1934)
This European car was the first front-wheel drive car in the world. It was made for twenty years without a change in design or engineering.

MERCEDES
The oldest car in commercial automotive history, it was first built in 1901 by auto inventor, Gottlieb Daimler of Germany. It was the first automobile to look like a car, not a horseless carriage. Daimler named this car after his daughter, Mercedes.

MOONCAR
The Apollo 15 mission to the moon introduced the moon car, also known as the lunar rover. It is an electric-powered four-wheel drive vehicle, which was developed at the cost of $60 million.

OLDSMOBILE
This was the first successful American-made car. Developed by Ranson Eli Olds in 1901, it still survives today.

MODEL T—'TIN LIZZIE'
Henry Ford's car, first introduced in 1908, made history when it rolled off the first-ever car assembly line in 1913. More than 15 million of these mass-produced cars were made.

VOLKSWAGEN 'BEETLE'
This German-made car is the best-selling car, ever. It was designed by Ferdinand Porsche in 1934 for the German dictator, Adolf Hitler. Hitler wanted a 'car for the people,' which is what the word *volkswagen* means.

MEMORABLE BICYCLES

THE PENNY FARTHING
Also known as the ordinary bike, had a large front wheel and a small back wheel. The rider pedalled cranks on the front wheel, turning the cranks in order to steer the bike. About 1870 wheels with steel instead of wooden spokes and solid rubber tyres were introduced.

THE ROVER SAFETY
Invented by the Englishman James Starley, this was one of the first bicycles with wheels of equal size and chain driven. It was mass-produced in 1885.

THE SWIFT LADIES
Made in 1926, this bike was unique because it was made without a crossbar so a woman wearing a skirt could easily get off and on the bike.

Air Travel

FIRST IN FLIGHT

1783 The first hot-air balloon took flight over France. The Montgolfier brothers, Jacques and Joseph, invented the balloon, which rose 6,000 feet and stayed aloft for 10 minutes.

1785 A Frenchman, Sebastian Lenormand, was the first to use a parachute when he jumped from the tower of the Montpelier Observatory in France.

1852 The first dirigible, a steam-powered balloon, was flown by Henri Giffard. The balloon travelled at a speed of 6.7 mph from Paris, France to Trappe, France.

1853 The first manned glider to succeed in flight soared 500 yards. The glider was built by Englishman Sir George Cayley who was 80 years old at the time. He sent his coachman aloft for the first flight.

1900 The first zeppelin (rigid-frame airship) took flight. Count Ferdinand von Zeppelin of Germany flew at a speed of 18 mph for 3½ miles.

1903 The first airplane flight took place in a biplane built by the American brothers Orville and Wilbur Wright. Because he won the toss of a coin, Orville was the first to make the flight. He travelled 120 feet in 12 seconds.

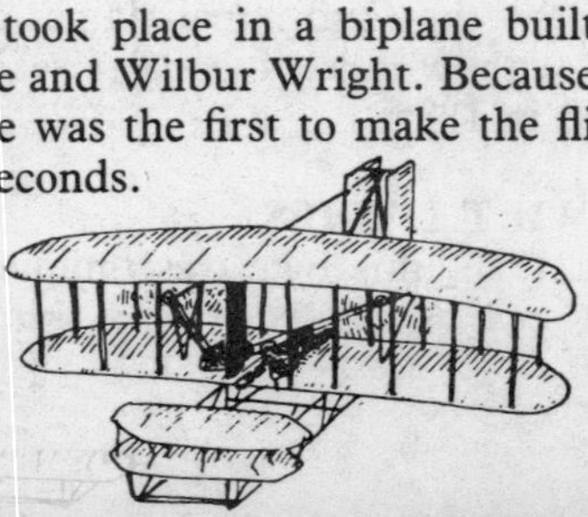

1911 The hydroplane (seaplane) was invented by Glenn Curtis of the U.S. The plane was designed to take off and to land on water.

1923 The first flight in a rotary-wing aircraft was made by Juan de la Cierva in Madrid, Spain.

1930 Jet-propelled aircraft was invented by Sir Frank Whittle of England.

FAMOUS AIRCRAFT

BOEING B-50A SUPERFORTRESS

This aircraft was the first to make a round-the-world non-stop flight. Captained by James Gallagher of the United States Air Force, it took off from Fort Worth, Texas on February 27, 1949. After 23,452 miles and four aerial refuellings, it landed in Fort Worth on March 2, 1949.

BOEING 747

The largest jumbo jet, this plane has a passenger capacity of 490. It is also notable for setting a speed record for around-the-world flight. From October 28 to October 31, 1977, it flew 26,382 miles over both the Earth's poles in 54 hours.

CONCORDE SST

This British-French aircraft was the first supersonic (faster than the speed of sound) transporter in commercial service. It carries 104 passengers at the speed of 1,300 mph. Its flight from Paris to New York takes 3 hours instead of the 6½ hours for an ordinary jet to travel the distance.

DE HAVILAND COMET

This British plane was the first pure jet airliner to go into commercial service in 1952.

EXPLORER I
The largest balloon to take flight, the *Explorer I*, had over 3 million cubit feet of surface area. In 1934, three men ascended in the balloon over the Black Hills of South Dakota. At 60,613 feet it exploded. The crew and equipment safely parachuted to earth.

FLYER
This biplane was flown by the Wright Brothers in their history-making flights over Kitty Hawk, North Carolina. In 1904 they made the first airplane manoeuvres; a turn and a complete circle, in the *Flyer*.

HINDENBERG
At 803-feet long, this was the largest dirigible ever built. It was made in Germany for transatlantic flight. After 35 successful trips across the ocean, it was destroyed by fire while trying to land in Lakehurst, New Jersey, in 1937. Thirty-six people died in the accident. No more of these aircraft were ever manufactured.

SPIRIT OF ST. LOUIS
When American Charles Lindbergh made the first solo transatlantic flight in this monoplane, it became one of the most famous planes ever. In 1927 Lindbergh took off from Roosevelt Field, Long Island, New York. Thirty-three hours, 39 minutes later, he safely landed 3,600 miles away in Le Bourget Field outside Paris, France.

WINNIE MAE
This Lockheed Vega was piloted by Wiley Post in the first round-the-world-solo flight. In 1933 Post travelled 15,596 miles around the world in 7 days, 18 hours, 49½ minutes.

SPRUCE GOOSE
This, the largest plane ever built, was designed and made by American millionaire, Howard Hughes. Made of wood, its wingspan is 320 feet. The only flight of this plane took place on November 2, 1947 when Hughes piloted it to a height of 70 feet for one mile. Today the plane is on exhibition in Long Beach, California.

Space Travel

FIRSTS

1961 The first person to travel in space was Yuri Gagarin, a Soviet cosmonaut. He travelled around the Earth on April 12, in *Vostok I*.

The first American in space was Alan Shepard, who made a suborbital 15-minute flight on May 5.

1962 The first American to orbit in space was John Glenn, who travelled around the Earth three times on February 20. His flight time was 4 hours, 55 minutes.

1965 The first person to walk in space was Alexei Leonov of the U.S.S.R., who spent 10 minutes outside his spacecraft on a tether.

1969 The first person to walk on the moon was American astronaut Neil Armstrong. On July 20, he put his left foot on the surface on the moon. He and fellow astronaut, Edwin Aldrin, spent two hours walking on the moon collecting samples of rocks and soil.

1972 *Pioneer 10* was the first spacecraft to pass through the asteroid belt between Mars and Jupiter. This proved that spacecraft could safely travel to the outer solar system. It was launched on March 3.

1975 The first time space crews from two different countries met and exchanged visits in space was July, 1975. The U.S. *Apollo 18* and the U.S.S.R. *Soyuz 19* met 145 miles above the Earth and docked in space. The U.S. astronauts were Thomas Stafford, Vance Brand, and Donald Slayton. The Soviet cosmonauts were Alexei Leonov and Valery Kubasov.

1981 The first re-usable spacecraft was the *Columbia* space shuttle launched by the U.S. on April 12. After orbiting the Earth 36 times, astronauts Robert Crippen and John Young successfully landed at Edwards Air Force Base in California on April 14.

1984 This space shuttle *Challenger* mission was one of 'firsts'. It had the first seven-person crew. It was the first time two women were aboard the same spacecraft (Sally Ride and Kathy Sullivan). It was the first time a U.S. woman (Ms. Sullivan) walked in space. It was the first demonstration of a satellite refuelling technique in space.

1986 The first space-probes explored Halley's Comet. The European satellite, *Giotto*, passed through the coma of the comet and transmitted photographs taken within 1000 km of the nucleus and a mass of new data.

U.S. SPACE MISSIONS

Manned Missions

MERCURY

The first manned space programme in the U.S. was called Project Mercury. It was designed to see if people could withstand the shock of launch, re-entry, and weightlessness in space. In 1963, astronaut Gordon Cooper spent more than 34 hours orbiting the earth in his spacecraft *Faith* 7. In doing so, he successfully proved people were capable of living and working in space.

GEMINI

This project was named from the Greek word *Gemini*, meaning 'twin'. These spacecraft were twice as large as those of the Mercury project and could accommodate two astronauts. The goal of this project was to see if people could live in space for long periods of time—two weeks or more. Walks in space and walks on the moon were part of the Gemini mission.

APOLLO

The goal of this project was to land a person on the Moon and return the person safely to Earth. The last three Apollo flights landed lunar rover vehicles. The astronauts used these to explore the surface of the Moon.

SKYLAB

This project successfully put a space station in orbit around the Earth. The working crew members proved that people could live in space for at least three months. Thousands of pictures were taken of the Earth and the Sun. Experimental animals spent time on board. They were studied to see how well they adapted to life in space.

SPACE SHUTTLE

The space shuttle *Columbia* was launched in 1981. It was a re-usable space transport designed to replace other U.S. launch vehicles as a cost-saving device. It can be used again for space transport, scientific exploration, and defence needs.

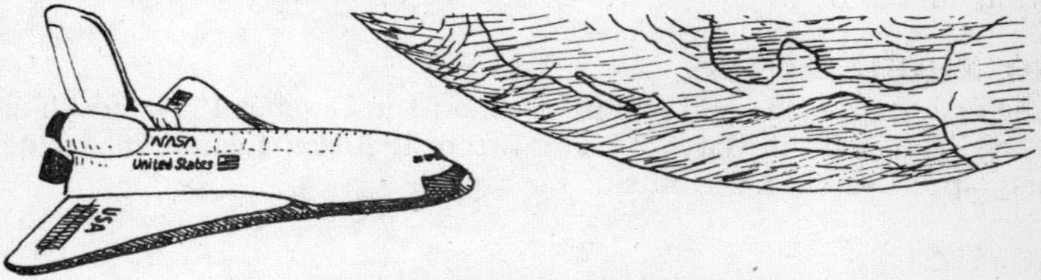

U.S. Planetary Unmanned Spacecraft

MARINER

Mariner 9 orbited Mars and sent back photographs of the planet in 1971. *Mariner* 10 bypassed Venus and Mercury in 1973.

PIONEER

In 1973 and 1974 *Pioneer 10* and *Pioneer 11* explored Jupiter and *Pioneer 11* also bypassed Saturn. *Pioneer Venus 1* and *Pioneer Venus* 2 explored Venus in 1978. *Pioneer 10* will be the first spacecraft to escape the solar system. By the 1990s, it will be 9 billion kilometres from the Sun.

VIKING

Viking 1 and *Viking 2* landed on the planet Mars in 1976 and sent back pictures of the red planet.

VOYAGER

Voyager 1 made the first detailed examination of Saturn in 1980, and in 1986 *Voyager 2* was the first space-probe to bypass Uranus Launched in 1977 it transmitted new information about the planet across 1,860 million miles. In August 1989 it will rendezvous with Neptune, 3000 million miles from Earth.

RUSSIAN SPACE MISSIONS

Manned Missions

VOSTOK

Vostok 1 was the first manned space-ship. In it, on April 12 1961, Yuri Gagarin completed an orbit round the Earth. On the following 6 August, Herman Titov in Vostok 2 made 17 orbits. In August 1962 Vostoks 3 and 4 were in orbit together. In June 1963 Valeri Bykovsky made 81 orbits in a 5-day journey in Vostok 5, while in the same month Valentina Tereshkova, the first woman astronaut, made 48 orbits in Vostok 6.

VOSKHOD

The first three-man flight was in Voskhod 1 in October 1964. Voskhod 2 was launched on March 18 1965; from it Alexei Leonov made the first 'space-walk', going outside his capsule.

SOYUZ

Many Soyuz flights have been made, starting with Soyuz 1 in April 1967; unfortunately the pilot, Komarov, was killed on landing. Later Soyuz vehicles have been used for transporting cosmonauts to and from space-stations, and for docking manoeuvres; Nos. 4 and 5 docked in 1969, and a few weeks later Soyuz 6, 7 and 8 also docked. With modifications and improvements Soyuz is still in service, achieving record duration voyages.

SALYUT

The first Salyut space-station was sent up in April 1971. Cosmonauts have stayed on board later Salyuts for many weeks. Salyut 7, launched in 1983, was still operational in 1986; it is serviced by Soyuz vehicles and carries out many experiments involving the use of telescopes, cameras and furnaces for processing materials.

MIR

Mir is intended to be the first permanent Russian space-station. It was launched in 1986 and will be extended by adding other spacecraft. It will include observatories, instruments for Earth Studies, biological laboratories and industrial equipment.

LITTLE KNOWN FACTS ABOUT SPACE TRAVEL

- America's *Skylab* was a 'space house' which resembled a small two-storey house in the suburbs. The first floor contained a workshop, a sleeping area, a kitchen, and a bathroom. The second floor was an experiment chamber where scientific tests were conducted.

- The L5 Society is a worldwide group of people who have dedicated themselves to being the first settlers in space.

- Twelve Americans have walked on the Moon.

- Three women have been in space: Soviet cosmonaut Valentina Tereshkova and U.S. astronauts Sally Ride and Kathryn Sullivan.

- The footprint left on the Moon by Neil Armstrong will stay there a very long time as there is no wind or water to disturb it.

- Astronauts have brought back to Earth 843 pounds of common rock.

- The space shuttle can go from the U.S. to Europe in less than 20 minutes.

- The U.S. space shuttle *Columbia* is 52 storeys high and is the world's largest (not tallest) 'building.' It covers 8 acres of space.

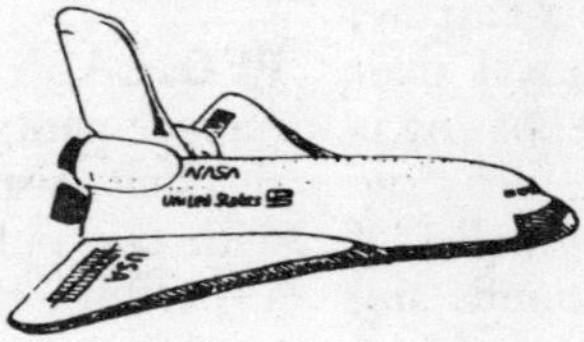

Transportation Centres

- An estimated 2.5 million bike trips take place each day in the city of Shanghai, China.
- Chicago International Airport at O'Hare Field is the world's busiest airport. Day and night, a landing or take-off occurs every 42 seconds.
- The world's largest railway station is Grand Central Station in New York City. The station covers 48 acres—the size of 37 football pitches. An average of 550 trains use the station's 67 tracks each day.

- The most extensive subway system in the world is in London. The Underground or 'tube' has 254 miles of track and 273 stations.
- The busiest subway system in the world is in New York City. More than 2 million people use the subways each work day.
- Land speed records are set at Bonneville Salt Flats in Utah.
- Mission Control for the United States space programme is in Houston, Texas.

Around the World

THE GONDOLA is a long, thin rowboat. It is used as a taxi in the canals of Venice, Italy. The gondolier uses a long, thin pole to push the boat through the canals.

AN ICEBOAT can move very fast with the wind. It is a narrow, pointed sailboat that moves over ice on three runners. Iceboating is a favourite pastime in the northern European countries of Norway, Denmark, Finland, and Sweden where sea, river, and lake water is frozen most of the year.

A JEEPNESS is a jitney bus of Manila, the Philippines. A jeepness is a brightly-decorated, converted jeep which holds 12 passengers.

A JUNK is a wooden sailboat used in the Orient. These boats have flat bottoms and high backs with two or more sails. They are usually painted in bright colours.

KAYAKS are long, painted canoes covered with sealskin. They are built with a small opening to fit the person who paddles it. For thousands of years, Eskimos of North America have been making and using kayaks.

PEDICABS are the modern replacements for rickshaws. A rickshaw was a two-wheeled cart with two poles in front pulled by a person. Rickshaws were first used in Asia in the late 1800s. The pedicap has two wheels on the back and one in the front. A driver sits on what looks like the

back half of a bicycle and pedals the cart around. Pedicabs are found in the cities of Southeast Asia.

SAMPANS are small boats found in China and Japan. They are used as homes for families, or as places of business—stores, restaurants, or small poultry farms.

Comparative Speeds of Selected Vehicles

Stagecoach	8 miles per hour
Early steam locomotive (Stephenson's Rocket)	15 miles per hour
Henry Ford's first car (Model T)	45 miles per hour
Snowmobile	135 miles per hour
Electric train	200 miles per hour
Supersonic transport (SST)	1,450 miles per hour
Rocketship	25,000 miles per hour (minimum to escape Earth's gravity)

Travel Talk

HOW FIVE VEHICLES WERE NAMED

BUS
This word is short for the Latin word *omnibus* which means 'for all'.

CLIPPER SHIP
This long, slender sailing ship of the 19th century was named for its speed. It was said to 'clip through the waves.'

HELICOPTER
When Leonardo da Vinci, the 16th-century artist/inventor first drew a design for a rotating wing machine, he called it a helix pteron, meaning 'spiral wing.' These Greek words were later written as 'helicopter'.

SCHOONER
This large sailboat was named after an 18th-century game known as 'schooning', whereby children skipped pebbles across the water.

TAXICAB
This word comes from a one-horse carriage called a cabriolet. This kind of carriage for hire had a taximeter inside which recorded the cost of the ride. Today, cars for hire are called taxicabs, cabs, or taxis.

The Universe

Get ready for the *space age* with this chapter which defines and explains what every future astronaut should know; from asteroids to stars, and how you can name your own comet.

A Guide to the Universe

WHAT IS WHAT IN THE UNIVERSE

Asteroid—A small rocky or metal object that revolves around the Sun. Most asteroids are found in the asteroid belt that lies between the planets Mars and Jupiter.

Black Hole—It is thought to be a massive collapsed star, which has a surrounding field of gravity so strong that neither light nor matter can escape from it.

Comet—A 'dirty snowball' of dust and ice which orbits the Sun. Comets have two tails, one of dust and one of gas.

Cosmos—Another word for the universe. All energy, matter, and space. Everything that exists.

Eclipse—A lunar eclipse occurs when the Sun, the Earth, and the Moon are in line and the Moon enters the Earth's shadow. A solar eclipse occurs when the Moon passes between the Sun and the Earth causing its shadow to fall upon the Earth.

Galaxy—A collection of billions of stars held together by gravitational force. There are at least 100 billion galaxies in the universe. Three are visible to the naked eye. They are: Andromeda, the Magellanic Cloud, and the Milky Way.

Light Year—The distance light travels in one year, which is approximately 6 trillion miles. The universe is measured in light years.

Meteor—A small particle, produced by a comet, orbiting the Sun. It can be seen only when it dashes into the Earth's upper air and burns away, producing the appearance of a shooting star.

Meteorite—A small body coming from space and landing on the Earth, sometimes making a crater. Meteorites are either stones or irons. There is probably no distinction between a large meteorite and a small asteroid.

Moon—A satellite that revolves around a planet. With the exception of Mercury and Venus, all the planets have moons.

Neutron Star—The core of a star left over after a supernova explodes.

Nova—A star which suddenly explodes and is temporarily bright.

Planet—A large rotating (turning) body that moves in orbit (revolves) around the Sun.

Pulsar—A rotating neutron star that emits beams of radiation.

Quasar—A starlike object which is extremely bright, small, and distant. Many quasars are sources of strong radio energy.

Star—A celestial body which gives off heat and light. Our local star is the Sun.

Supernova—A tremendous stellar explosion, indicating the death of a massive star. For a few days, weeks or months a supernova may shine 15,000,000 times as brilliantly as the Sun.

OUR PLACE IN THE UNIVERSE

We live in the Milky Way galaxy. Our solar system and a spiral-shaped system of 120 billion stars are part of the Milky Way. It would take 100,000 light years to travel from one end of our galaxy to the other.

Our solar system is made up of one star, the Sun, nine known planets, fifty-seven known moons, more than 30,000 asteroids, an estimated 100 billion comets, and a large amount of interplanetary 'dust'.

FACTS ABOUT THE SUN

- The Sun is a 5 billion-year-old star which, it is estimated, will continue to exist for another 5 billion years.
- The Sun is an average-size star. There are much larger stars in the universe.
- 109 Earths would fit side by side across the diameter of the Sun.
- The Sun spins on its axis from left to right.
- The Sun is not a ball of fire. It is more like a huge hydrogen bomb that is continuously exploding and giving off energy and light.

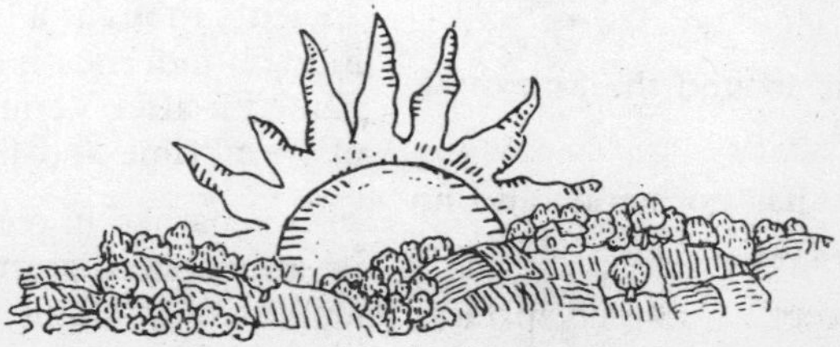

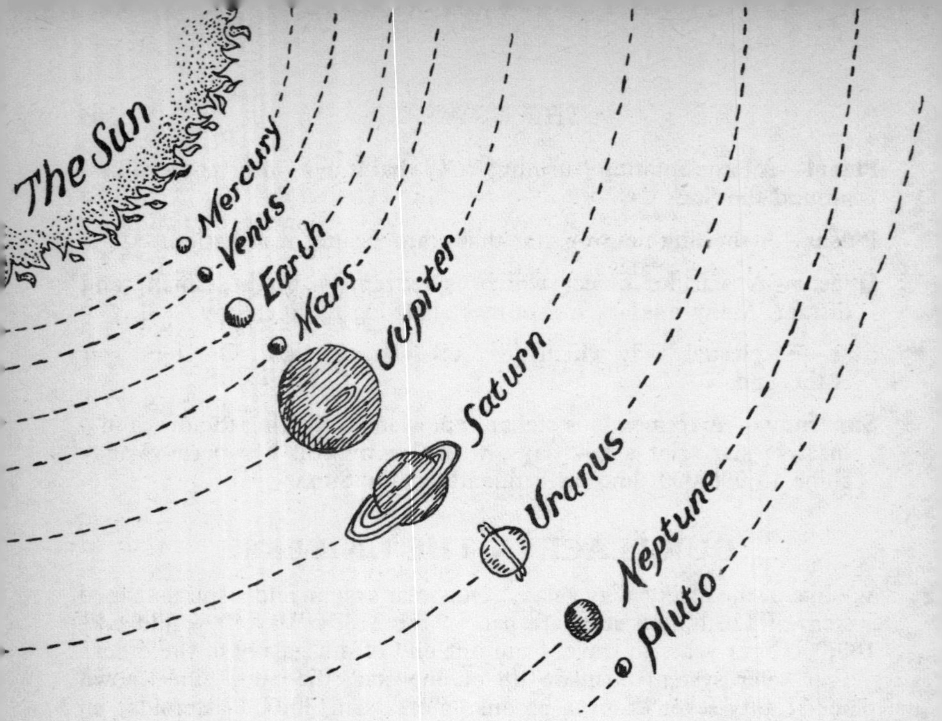

FACTS ABOUT THE PLANETS

Mercury, Venus, Earth, and Mars all have solid surfaces. Jupiter, Saturn, Uranus, and Neptune all are fluid bodies made of gas or liquid.

MERCURY

- It was named after Mercury, the speedy messenger of the Roman gods.
- It is the swiftest-moving planet.
- It is the planet closest to the Sun.
- It travels around the Sun in 88 Earth days.
- Mercury has no moons and no atmosphere (air).
- It has a rocky, cratered surface.
- It has a rotation period of 58½ times as long as our 'day'.

VENUS

- This planet was once called the 'Planet of Mystery' because of the cloud-like veil that covers it. The ancients thought a lush world was hidden underneath the veil and so named it after Venus, the goddess of springtime and flowers.
- It is bathed in red light because its atmosphere scatters red wave-lengths of sunlight.

• On Venus, lightning flashes and thunder roars day and night.

• This planet spins so slowly that it takes 243 Earth days to make one full turn.

• It takes 224.7 Earth days for Venus to revolve around the Sun.

EARTH

• It is called in Latin, *Terra Mater*, Earth Mother of humans.

• It is the only planet known to sustain forms of life.

• This is a planet covered more by water than by land.

• It travels around the Sun in 365 days.

• The same side of the Moon always faces the Earth.

• The Moon shines because it reflects the light of the Sun.

• A full Moon is when sunlight reflects against the side of the Moon facing us on Earth.

• It takes 27 days for the Moon to travel around the Earth.

MARS

• Known as the angry red planet, Mars was named for the Roman god of war.

• It is red in colour because of its rustlike soil which is coated with iron oxide.

• It is known for its severe dust storms.

• There are canyons, volcanic mountains, frozen water, and ice caps of carbon dioxide (dry ice) on this planet.

• It takes 687 Earth days for Mars to travel around the Sun.

JUPITER

• It is called the 'King of Planets' and was named after the king of the Roman gods.

• It is the largest planet, a giant which weighs more than all the other planets put together.

• It has more moons than any other planet, with at least 17 moons of which three are larger than our Moon.

• Its famous Great Red Spot is a hurricane-like storm, larger than the Pacific Ocean, that has been raging for centuries.

• Jupiter travels around the Sun in 11.86 Earth years.

SATURN

• This planet was named for the Roman god of farming.

• It is famous for its 7 main rings made up of icy particles; some tiny, others as large as buildings.

- It is yellow in colour.
- It takes 29.46 Earth years to travel around the Sun.

URANUS

- Uranus was the Roman god who was the father of Saturn and the grandfather of Jupiter.
- It is bluish-green in colour.
- It has black rings around it which are thought to be made of chunks of dark rock.
- This planet is unusual in that it lies almost on its side.
- It travels around the Sun in 84 Earth years.

NEPTUNE

- Because of its ocean colour it was named for Neptune, the Roman god of water.
- It has two moons, one which orbits the planet in a year; the other completes its orbit in 6 days, moving backwards.
- It is pale blue in colour.
- Like Jupiter and Saturn it radiates more energy than it receives from the Sun.
- It travels around the Sun every 164¾ years.

PLUTO

- It was named for Pluto, the god who ruled the underworld.
- It has a large moon, Charon, which is very close in distance to Pluto, causing some to think it might be a double planet.
- It is on average the planet farthest from the Sun; 3,658 million miles away.
- Its unusual orbit causes Pluto to come closer to the Sun than its neighbour, Neptune, at certain points in time—as between 1979 and 1999.
- One year on Pluto is equal to 248 Earth years.

Have You Ever Wondered?

1. **What is the brightest star?** Sirius, which is 50 billion miles away, is the brightest-appearing star.

2. **What is a shooting star?** It is another name for a meteor.

3. **How are comets named?** They are usually named after their discoverers. For example, Halley's comet, which appears every 76

years and last reappeared in 1986, was named after Edmond Halley of England. Halley was the first to predict the reappearance of a comet.

4. What is a constellation? It is a nonscientific name for a group of stars. Some of the imaginary shapes of constellations are humans, real-life animals, and legendary beasts such as dragons and unicorns.

5. How old is the moon? It is as old as the Earth, which is at least 4.6 million years old.

6. Which planet was the only one discovered in the 20th century? Pluto, by Clyde Tombaugh in 1930 at the Lowell Observatory in Arizona.

7. What was the first planet visited by a spacecraft from Earth? Venus, by the U.S. spacecraft *Mariner* 2 in 1962.

8. What is the distance of the moon from the Earth? The Moon is 239,000 miles away. Its distance is equal to 9 times around the Earth's equator.

9. How many stars are in the known universe? About 100 sextillion. (Counting all known stars at a rate of 10 stars per second, it would take 100,000 times longer than the universe has been known to exist.)

The World and Weather

Here are hundreds of odd and fascinating facts about the entire world—from the largest continent to the smallest, from the coldest place to the driest—cities, mountains, rivers, countries, oceans—you name it.

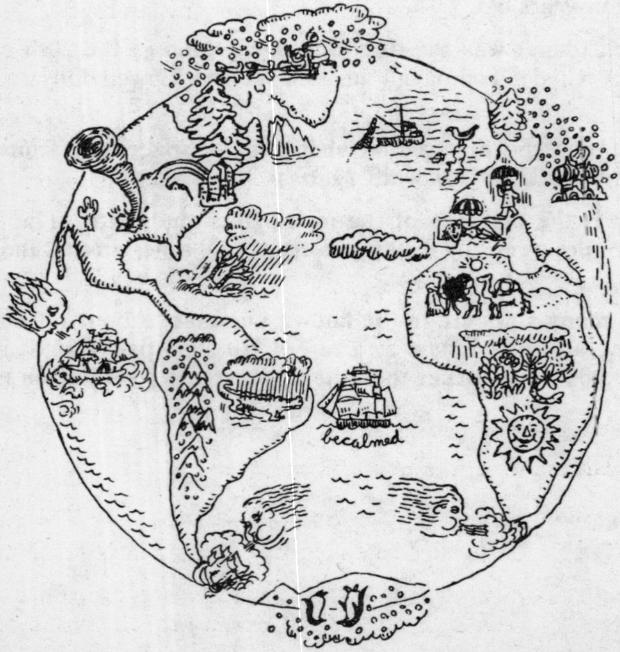

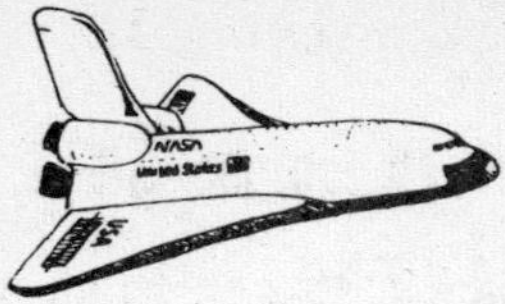

A Profile of the Earth

- The Earth is the fifth largest planet in the solar system.
- It is approximately 93 million miles from the Sun. It would take a jet plane a little over 21 years to reach the sun at 500 mph.
- It is pear shaped and 'fattest' just below the equator.
- A jet plane can fly around the Earth in less than a day.
- An astronaut can circle the Earth in a rocket ship in 90 minutes.
- About 70 percent of the Earth's surface is covered by water.
- The greatest percentage of land lies north of the equator.
- The 'four corners' of the Earth are made by four bulges located in Ireland, near Peru, just south of Africa, and near New Guinea.
- The largest ocean is the Pacific.
- The largest continent is Asia.
- The highest point on the Earth is Mount Everest in Nepal-Tibet.
- The lowest point on the Earth is the Dead Sea in Israel/Jordan.
- The largest sea is the South China Sea.
- The longest river is the Nile.
- The largest freshwater lake is Lake Superior in North America.
- The deepest ocean point is the Mariana's Trench, which is 35,810 feet deep. It is located in the Pacific Ocean near the island of Guam.

- The highest waterfall is Angel Falls in Venezuela, measuring 3,281 feet about $^{2}/_{3}$ of a mile high.
- The largest desert is the Sahara in Africa. It covers 3,320,000 square miles almost as large as the entire United States.
- The largest island is Greenland. Located in the North Atlantic, it covers 839,999 square miles, 9 times the size of the United Kingdom.

Continents

NORTH AMERICA

North America is the third largest continent.

The world's largest group of fresh water lakes are located in North America. They are the Great Lakes.

North America has the longest coastline of any continent. It is 96,000 miles long.

Population: 390 million
Size: 9,366,000 square miles
Highest Point: Mt. McKinley, Alaska; 20,320 feet above sea level, almost 4 miles high
Lowest Point: Death Valley, California; 282 feet below sea level
Largest Country: Canada; 3,851,787 square miles
Most Populous Country: United States; 232 million

SOUTH AMERICA

South America is the fourth largest continent.

The world's longest mountain range, the Andes, is in South America. The Andes mountains are 15,000 miles long.

Most of the people of South America live along the coastline of the continent.

The southernmost city in the world, Punta Arenas, Chile, is located in South America.

Population: 259 million (approximately)
Size: 6,881,000 square miles

Highest Point: Mt. Aconcagua, Argentina; 22,834 feet above sea level, about 4 1/3 miles high
Lowest Point: Salinas Grande, Argentina; 131 feet below sea level
Largest Country: Brazil; 3,286,470 square miles
Most Populous Country: Brazil; 127,700,000

EUROPE

Europe is the second smallest continent.

The largest ice cave in the world is located in Europe. It is the Eisriesenwelt Cave in Austria.

Population: 692,879,000
Size: 4,017,000 square miles
Highest Point: Mt. Elbrus, Russia; 18,510 feet above sea level, about 3½ miles high
Lowest Point: Caspian Sea; 92 feet below sea level
Largest Country: U.S.S.R.; 8,649,490 square miles
Most Populous Country: U.S.S.R.; 268,800,000

AFRICA

It is the second largest continent.

Africa is the warmest continent in the world.

There are 48 countries on the continent of Africa; which makes it the continent with the most countries.

Population: 513 million
Size: 11,688,000 square miles
Highest Point: Mt. Kibo, Kilimanjaro in Tanzania; 19,340 feet above sea level, about 3½ miles high
Lowest Point: Lake Assal, Djibouti; 510 feet below sea level
Largest Country: Sudan; 967,000 square miles
Most Populous Country: Nigeria; 82,300,000

ASIA

Asia covers one-third of the Earth's land surface.

It is the world's largest continent.

More than one half of the people in the world live in Asia.

Five of the longest rivers in the world are located in Asia. They are the Yangtze, Yensei, Yellow, Irtysh and Amur rivers.

The highest point and the lowest point in the world are in Asia.

Population: 2 thousand million (approximately)
Size: 17,139,455 square miles
Highest Point: Mt. Everest, Nepal-Tibet; 29,028 feet above sea level, about 5½ miles high
Lowest Point: Dead Sea, Israel/Jordan; 1,296 feet below sea level, about 1½ miles below sea level

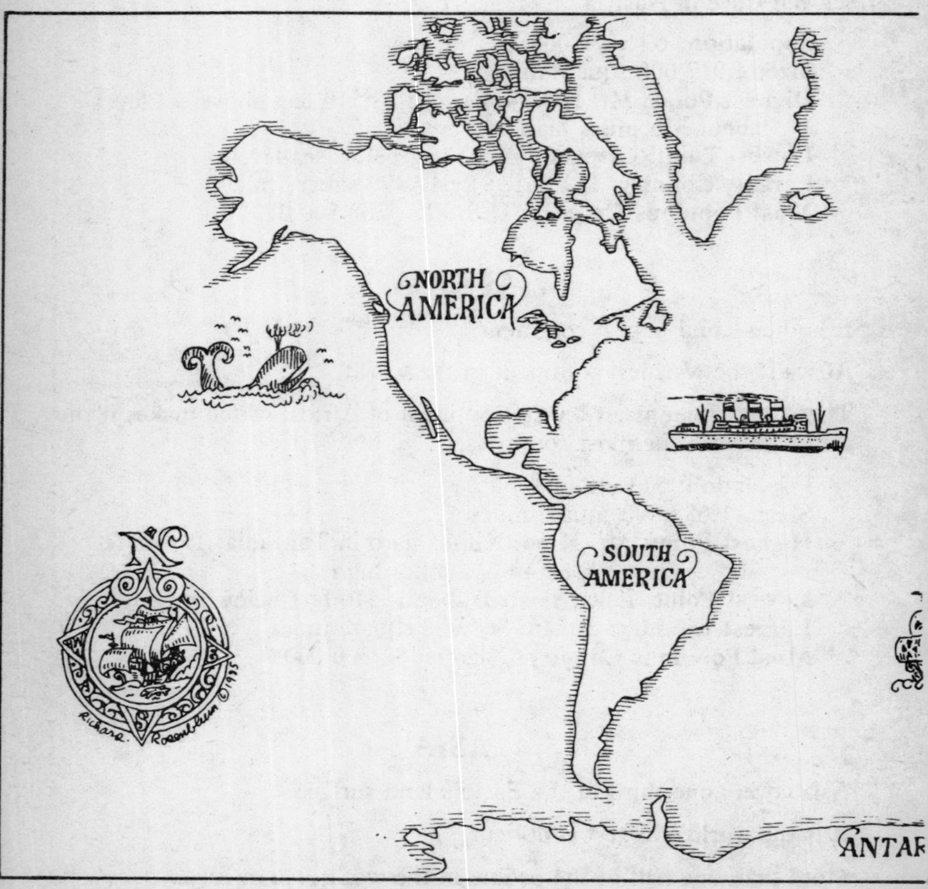

Largest Country: China, 3,769,000 square miles
Most Populous Country: China; 1 thousand million (approximately)

OCEANIA

This continent includes many islands in the Pacific, as well as Australia, New Zealand and Papua New Guinea.

Ninety percent of the land mass is the island of Australia.

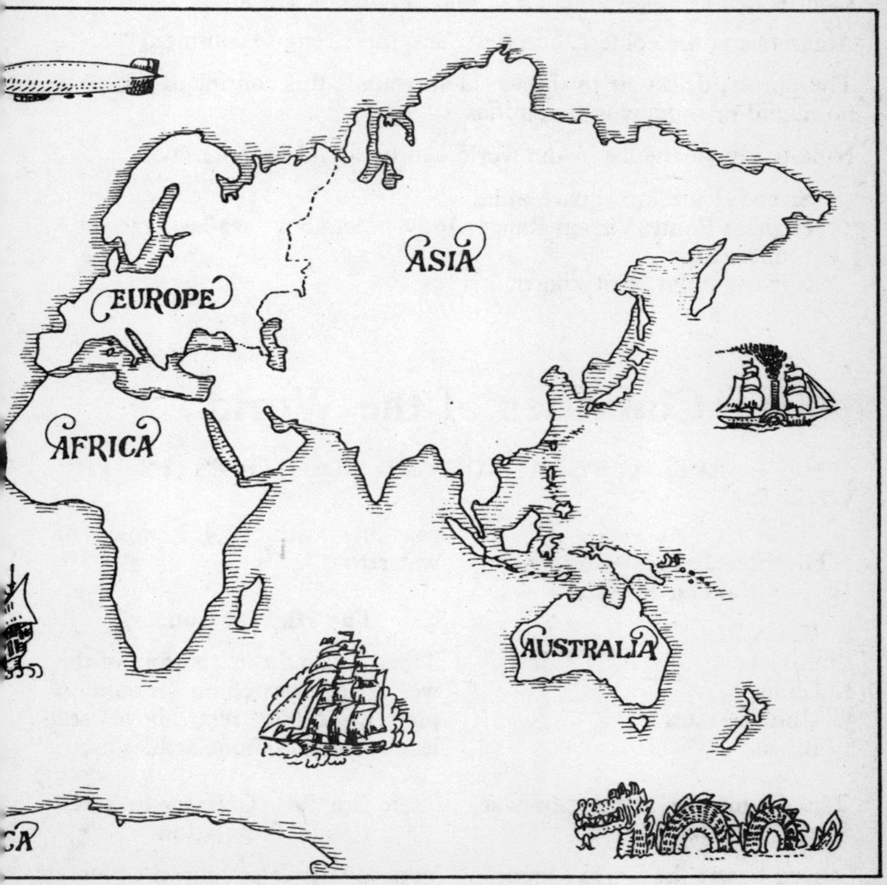

Population: 23 million; (Australia: 15 million)
Size: 8,5000,000 square miles: (Australia: 7,686,000 square miles)
Highest Point: Jaja Peak, West Irian, New Guinea; 16503 feet above sea level, about 3 miles
Lowest Point: Lake Eyre, South Australia; 36 feet below sea level.

ANTARCTICA

The fifth largest continent is Antarctica.

Antarctica is the world's highest continent. It is covered by an ice sheet which averages a height of one mile above sea level.

Antarctica is the coldest, emptiest, and most remote continent.

The purest, driest air in the world surrounds this continent. There is no mould or mildew in Antarctica.

Nine-tenths of the ice in the world can be found in Antarctica.

Size: 5.1 million square miles
Highest Point: Vinson Range; 16,864 feet above sea level, about 3 miles high
Lowest Point: Not known

Countries of the World

(THERE ARE A TOTAL OF 215 COUNTRIES IN THE WORLD.)

The Five Largest Countries Ranked by Size

1. U.S.S.R.
2. Canada
3. China
4. United States
5. Brazil

The Country with the Longest Coastline

Canada boasts the world's longest coastline with 56,453 miles of waterfront.

The Highest Country

Tibet is called the 'rooftop' of the world. It is located on a mountain plateau 15,000 feet above sea level, which is about 3 miles high.

The Smallest Country in Size and Population

Vatican City (also known as State

of Vatican City) in Europe covers 0.17 square miles. It has a population of approximately 1000.

The Five Most Populous Countries

1. China
2. India
3. U.S.S.R.
4. United States
5. Indonesia

The Country with the Most Lakes and Rivers

Canada—8.29 percent is covered by water, of which 755,165 sq. kilometres are lakes and rivers.

The Poorest Country in the World

Bangladesh, where more people live in poverty than anywhere else.

The Countries with the Highest Literacy Rates

These 8 countries claim that 99.5 percent of their people over the age of 12 can read a simple sentence and write basic information about themselves.

Bermuda	Naura
Czechoslovakia	South Africa
Macao	United States
Monaco	Vatican City

How Many Under-15s in the World

It is estimated* that there are 1,700 million children under the age of 15. By the year 2,000 there will be 2,100 million. The breakdown of percentages of kids in selected countries of the world is as follows:

Country	*% of Population 15 and under*		*% of Population 15 and under*
Australia	25	Mexico	42
Bolivia	44	Nigeria	48
China	34	U.K.	20
India	39	U.S.A.	22
Kenya	52	U.S.S.R.	25

**United Nations Demographic Yearbook, 1983*

Countries and Communications

The following is a list of countries with the greatest number of items per person. They are ranked in order.

Daily Newspapers	*Radios*	*Telephones*	*Televisions*
U.S.	U.S.	U.S.	U.S.
India	Canada	Sweden	Kuwait
U.S.S.R.	Australia	Switzerland	Denmark

A Profile of the U.S.

The United States is the fourth largest country in the world.
The U.S.:

- Owns one half of the world's wealth.
- Has the largest government budget in the world.
- Has the largest postal service in the world.
- Produces the greatest amount of meat and coal in the world.
- Uses more energy than any other country.
- Uses more cars than any other country.
- Sells more candy and soda pop than any other country.

POPULATION FACTS

The total world population increases by 2 percent each year. It is estimated that by the year 2,000 there will be over 6,000 million people living in the world.

Every year, for the next 30 to 40 years, the world will have to find room for, on average, an additional 85 million people.

In theory the world could produce enough food for everyone, but a recent study by the United Nations indicates that by the year 2,000, thirty-six countries will still be unable to feed their population from their own land.

By the year 2,000 the 'developing' countries will have needed to find work for 676 million new entrants to their labour forces.

The United Kingdom is one of the most densely populated countries in the world, but the population will probably have increased by one million by the year 2,000.

The number of people over 64 years of age in the world is estimated at 290 million. This will increase to 369 million by the year 2,000, and 465 million by the year 2,200.

The number of people in Europe (exclude the USSR) is 492 million. Those of 'working age' (approximately 270 million) have to support 221 million young and elderly.

Cities of the World

Most Populous City: Mexico City, Mexico has an estimated population of 14,750,000.

Highest City: Lhasa, Tibet (12,087 feet above sea level, or about 2¼ miles).

Highest Capital: La Paz, Bolivia (12,001 feet above sea level).

Oldest Existing City: Damascus, Syria, inhabited since prehistoric times.

Most Expensive City in which to Live: Tokyo, Japan.

A Divided City: Before WW II, Berlin was the capital of Germany. Today the city lies within the borders of East Germany but a wall divides it into East Berlin and West Berlin. East Berlin is part of East Germany; West Berlin is a city of West Germany.

A Buried City: The ancient city of Pompeii, Italy, was buried under ash and rock when the volcano, Mt. Vesuvius, erupted in 79 A.D. For 1,600 years it was forgotten. Then, in 1789, an Italian farmer was digging a well and discovered the buried city. When archaeologists uncovered the city, they found homes, public buildings, and shops still standing.

A Lost City: Machu Picchu was once an important Inca city located high in the Andes mountains of Peru. The city was thought to be the last stronghold of the Incas against the invasion of the Spanish conquistadores. For generations it was a guarded secret. In 1911, Hiram Bingham, an archaeologist from Yale University, found the once-lost city.

A Winter City Without Furnaces: Reykjavik, Iceland, is a cold northern city. The people who live there do not have stoves or furnaces to heat their homes. Instead, they use the hot water which is heated by the earth and found in abundance in springs and geysers under their city.

A City Within a City: The Kremlin is a wall-enclosed city of government buildings, palaces, churches, and museums within the city of Moscow, U.S.S.R.

Holiday Cities: Loveland, Colorado is known as 'America's Sweetheart City'. On Valentine's Day of each year, millions of Americans mail their love notes from this city so they will be postmarked 'from Loveland'. Santa Claus, Indiana is a city where the spirit of Christmas is always alive. A large statue of Santa stands in the centre of the city.

The Southernmost City in the World: Punta Arenas at the tip of Chile in South America is further south than any other city in the world.

One City from Two: Budapest is the capital city of Hungary. Before 1872, Buda and Pest were separate cities. Buda was the original capital of Hungary (1371). By the early 1800s, Pest, the city across the Danube River from Buda, had become a more important city. The people of Hungary made the two cities one and called their capital Budapest.

THE HOLY PLACES OF WORLD RELIGIONS

Benares, India	Hinduism
Buddh Gaya, India	Buddhism

Jerusalem, Israel	Christianity, Judaism and Islam
Kiev, Russia	Russian Orthodox
Mecca, Saudi Arabia	Islam
Fuji Yama, Japan	Shintoism

CITIES AND THEIR NICKNAMES

Chicago	'The Windy City'	Located on Lake Michigan, it is subject to frequent stiff breezes.
Los Angeles	'The City of Angels'	Los Angeles is Spanish for 'City of Angels'.
Minneapolis St. Paul	'The Twin Cities'	These two cities were built next to each other. Only the Missisippi River, which flows between the two cities, separates them.
New York	'The Big Apple'	Jazz musicians touring the country in the 1920s had a saying: 'There are many apples on the tree but to play New York is to play the Big Time—"The Big Apple" '.

Paris	'The City of Lights'	Paris was the first European city to have street lights.

Philadelphia	'City of Brotherly Love'	In Greek, philadelphia means 'brotherly love'.
Rome	'The Eternal City'	The ancient Romans thought their city was the centre of an eternal universe.
Venice	'Bride of the Sea'	Venice, Italy, is built on 118 islands in the Adriatic Sea.

Oceans and Seas

OCEANS

Oceans Ranked By Size

Pacific	63,800,000 square miles.
Atlantic	31,700,000 square miles, about half the size of the Pacific.
Indian	28,350,500 square miles.
Arctic	5,425,000 square miles.

Deepest Ocean

- The Pacific Ocean has an average depth of 14,000 feet, or just over 2½ miles.

Shrinking and Growing Oceans

- Every year the Atlantic Ocean grows wider by an inch or so. Every year the Pacific shrinks by an inch or so. This is due to the movement of the Earth's surface.

An Ocean to Walk Across

- In winter, the Arctic Ocean forms a 10-foot ice cover linking the United States and Russia.

Ocean of Commerce

• The Atlantic is the busiest ocean for commercial trade.

Ocean of Monsoons

• The Indian Ocean is known for seasonal wind and rain storms which are called the monsoons.

Ocean of Oil

• The Indian Ocean is the world's greatest source of offshore oil. More than 40 percent of all offshore oil comes from this ocean.

Saltiest Ocean

• The Mediterranean Ocean has the greatest density of salt at an average salinity rate of 39 percent.

Ocean Names

• The Pacific was named by the Spanish explorer, Ferdinand Magellan. When Magellan sailed on the Pacific it was calm and peaceful. The Spanish word for peaceful is *pacifico*.

• The Atlantic was named by the ancient Romans. They thought the Atlas Mountains in Africa were the end of the earth's land. They named the ocean on the other side of the mountains Atlantic.

SEAS

The Four Largest Seas

South China	1,148,500 square miles
Caribbean Sea	971,400 square miles
Mediterranean Sea	969,100 square miles
Bering Sea	873,000 square miles

How Five Seas Were Named

The Black Sea is landlocked between Europe and Asia. It has a high concentration of hydrogen sulphide, a deadly gas which colours the sea floor black.

The Dead Sea was given its name because no fish live in it and very few plants grow in it. This is because its water is extremely salty.

The Red Sea was so named because the coral reefs, seaweed, and tiny sea animals that live in this sea are red.

The White Sea is north of the U.S.S.R. Most of the year it is covered by ice and snow.

The Yellow Sea was named for the yellow mud carried by the rivers which empty into it.

Mountains

FAMOUS MOUNTAIN PEAKS

ADAM'S PEAK in Sri Lanka is a mountain considered to be sacred by three religious groups; Buddhists, Hindus, and Moslems.

MAUNA KEA in Hawaii is the tallest mountain peak measuring from its seabed to its peak. It is 33,476 feet high. Only 13,796 feet, or less than half of the mountain, is above ground.

MT. ARARAT located near the Turkish-Iranian border is, according to the *Bible*, the place where Noah's ark rested after the rains subsided.

MT. FUJI in Japan is the most photographed and painted mountain in the world.

MT. EVEREST, the highest mountain in the world, on the Tibet-Nepal border, was first climbed by Edmund Hillary and Tenzing Norgay in 1953.

MT. OLYMPUS, the highest mountain peak in Greece, was known as the 'home of the gods' to the ancient Greeks.

MT. RUSHMORE in the Black Hills of South Dakota is noted for its gigantic sculpture of four U.S. presidents. The heads of George Washington, Thomas Jefferson, Abraham Lincoln, and Teddy Roosevelt have been carved in 70-foot-high likenesses. It took John Borglum and his son, Lincoln, fourteen years to carve the sculpture.

MT. SINAI located, in Egypt is, according to the *Bible*, the mountain-top where Moses received the Ten Commandments.

MT. VESUVIUS in Italy erupted and destroyed the City of Pompeii in 79 A.D. Today, it is the only active volcano on the continent of Europe.

RECORD BOOK MOUNTAINS

Tallest Mountain Range: The Himalaya mountain range contains 96 of the world's 109 tallest peaks.

Tallest Underwater Mountain Range: The Cordillera, which is in the Indian and East Pacific Oceans. Its average height is 8,000 feet above the base ocean depth.

Longest Mountain Range: The Andes in South America. They are 15,000 miles long.

Richest Mountain Range: The Andes are the most abundant mountain source of gold, silver, copper, and other valuable minerals.

Highest Mountain Peak: Mt. Everest in the Himalayas, Tibet-Nepal. It is 29,028 feet above sea level or about 5½ miles high.

Highest Island Mountain Peak: Jaja Peak, West Irian, New Guinea; which is 16,503 feet above sea level or about 3 miles high.

Largest Volcanic Mountain: Mauna Loa in Hawaii is 13,680 feet high, with a crater 3 miles long and 1½ miles wide.

Rivers

THE WORLD'S LONGEST AND MOST FAMOUS RIVER
The Nile River in Africa starts in the tributaries of Lake Victoria, travels north for 4,145 miles, then empties into the Mediterranean Sea.

It flows through the 'cradle of civilization', past the world famous pyramids of Egypt. For centuries the Nile has given life to a rainless land. Although it passes through desert lands, its river valley is one of the most fertile farming areas in the world.

THE MIGHTIEST RIVER

There is more water in the Amazon River of South America than in any other river in the world. It carries one-fifth of the world's running water; three thousand million gallons a day. The Amazon is so powerful that it pushes its fresh water 200 miles out to sea, where it empties into the Atlantic Ocean.

'THE FATHER OF WATERS'

The Mississippi, the great American river, has earned its nickname. It begins as a tiny stream (only six steps across) in Lake Itasca, Minnesota, widens to a mile across where it joins the Ohio River, then ends its 2,348-mile journey at the Gulf of Mexico. The Mississippi with its tributaries passes through 31 states, providing America with 15,000 miles of transport waterways. It is America's river of music, folklore, history, and adventure.

'CHINA'S HIGH STREET'

The Yangtze is the chief river of China. The people of China call it 'The River' for it is their life stream. It is a trade river; half the commerce of all China travels on the Yangtze. It is also an agricultural river, irrigating millions of farms. One-tenth of mankind depends on the Yangtze as a means of transportation and as a source of food.

'THE RIVER OF FAITH'

Millions of Hindus consider the Ganges River in India to be holy water. They bathe in it to wash away their sins. They have built temples near its headwaters, high in the Himalayan Mountains. They sprinkle the ashes of their dead into it to ensure the dead's salvation.

'THE RIVER THAT FLOWS TWO WAYS'

The American Indian called the Hudson River of New York 'shatemuc,' which means 'the river that flows two ways'. The name was later changed to the Hudson in honour of the European explorer, Henry Hudson. The Hudson river is known for the strong incoming ocean tides which push salt water 150 miles upstream. When the tides recede, the water flows back into the ocean. This gives the appearance of a river which flows both north and south.

THE RIVER OF DIAMONDS

The Orange River in South Africa might be considered the richest river in the world. It carries diamonds as it flows. The diamonds are deposited along the riverbanks where they can be picked by hand. Today, a mining company owns the valuable rights to the diamonds in this river.

'BACKWARD'-FLOWING RIVER

The Chicago River in Illinois once emptied into Michigan. Because of industrial pollutants in the river, engineers rerouted it with a series of canals. It now flows the opposite way, into the Mississippi.

Lakes

World's Largest Salt Water Lake: The Caspian Sea in the U.S.S.R., which is 760 miles long, with a total area of 143,244 square miles.

World's Largest Freshwater Lake: Lake Superior in North America, which covers 31,700 square miles.

World's Largest Underground Lake: The lost sea in the Craighead caverns in Sweetwater, Tennessee. It covers 4½ acres.

Largest Lake in the U.K.: Lough Neagh in Northern Ireland covers 389 sq. km.

World's Deepest Lake: Lake Baykal in Siberia, U.S.S.R. It is 5,315 feet deep.

World's Highest Lake: Lake Titicaca in Peru/Bolivia, South America is 12,500 feet above sea level. It is the highest lake in the world that can be navigated by steam powered engines. An unnamed lake near Mt. Everest is 19,300 feet high but not navigable.

World's Most Polluted Lake: Lake Erie, one of the Great Lakes of North America, has the greatest amount of oil-soaked debris and industrial pollution.

Largest Man-made Lake in the U.S.: Lake Mead on the Arizona/Nevada border covers 28,700 acres. It is the result of the Hoover Dam.

Deserts

• Approximately 1⅞ percent of the world's land is covered by desert.

• Every continent in the world has deserts except Europe.

• The largest desert in the world is the Sahara in northern Africa. It covers 3,320,000 square miles.

• The hottest desert is the Libyan Sahara where the temperature in the shade has been recorded as high as 58°C (136.5°F).

• The sandiest desert in the world is the Arabian Desert in Africa.

• The highest desert in the world is the Atacama in northern Chile. It is 13,500 feet above sea level at its highest point.

Caves

• Scientists who study caves are called speleologists.

• The sport of cave exploring is called 'spelunking'.

• The longest cave system in the world is the Mammoth Cave in Kentucky, U.S.A. which is 150 miles long. Connecting with the Flint Ridge Cave system the total length is 301 miles (484 km).

• The largest cave in the world is the Sarawak Chamber in the Gunung Mulu National Park, Sarawak. It is 200 metres (2,300 ft) long, 300 metres (980 ft) wide, and its height is never less than 70 metres (230 ft).

• The deepest cave in Europe is the Gouffre Jean Bernard Cave in France. It is 1,535 metres (5,036 ft) deep.

• The deepest caves in Britain are the Ogof Ffynnon, in Wales which is 308 metres (1,010 ft) deep, and Giant's Hole System in England which is 214 metres (702 ft) deep.

• The longest cave system in Britain is the Ease Gill System, of which 32.5 miles (52.4 km) have been explored.

Ten Earthquake Facts

1. The earth shakes when it releases energy. These tremors are called earthquakes.

2. About a half million earthquakes are detected by scientists each year.

3. Scientists who study earthquakes are called seismologists.

4. Seismologists have drawn two 'earthquake belts' around the earth. These are the areas where earthquakes occur most frequently.

5. In 132 A.D., a Chinese mathematician devised the first instrument to measure earthquakes.

6. Today, earthquakes are measured on a scale of 1 to 9. The scale was devised by Dr. Charles Richter of the California Institute of Technology. It is called the Richter scale. This is a simple explanation of what the numbers on the Richter scale mean.

1—Felt by scientific instruments only.
2—Felt by very sensitive people and some animals.
3—Felt by most people.
4—Felt by all people.
5—Walls may crack, household objects fall.
6—Structures like chimneys may tumble. Destructive in populated areas.
7—A major quake in which lives are lost and buildings destroyed.
8—A disaster.
9—No earthquake has yet measured 9 on this scale.

7. The worst earthquake in world history took place in China on January 23, 1556. The death toll was 830,000.

8. The worst earthquake in North America took place in Alaska on March 27, 1964. It measured 8.5 on the Richter scale.

9. The worst year for recorded earthquakes was 1976. Major tremors occurred in China, Guatemala, Indonesia, Italy, the

Philippines, the U.S.S.R., and Turkey.

10. Giant waves caused by earthquakes are called tsunami, not tidal waves. Tsunami can travel at speeds of 500 mph. The largest recorded tsunami was 278 feet high. It appeared off southwest Alaska after a 1964 earthquake there.

Legendary Creatures of the Earth

THE ABOMINABLE SNOWMAN

The Abominable Snowman, also known as the Yeti, is said to live in the Himalayan Mountains of Asia. The natives of the Himalayas firmly believe that the Yeti is a magical creature who walks on two legs, moving about during the night and sleeping throughout the day. The Yeti has been described as a tall ape-like figure covered with hair. Its head is pointed and its mouth and teeth extremely large. It is said to have a loud roar, an unusual odour, and eats other animals for food.

Only a handful of westerners have claimed sightings of this creature. However, in 1951, Eric Shipton, a mountain climber, took photographs of what was supposedly the Yeti's footprint. These photos have kept the mystery of the Abominable Snowman alive in the western world.

The people of the Himalayas consider the Yeti a real creature, not a mythical one. For example, in 1958 the country of Nepal placed the Yeti on a protected species list. In the country of Bhutan the Yeti is the national animal and stamps with pictures of this creature have been issued.

BIGFOOT

Bigfoot is the legendary creature of North America. It's also known as the Sasquatch, a name given by the Salish Indians of Canada, which means 'wild man of the woods'. In 1811, mysterious footprints of this creature were found in the Canadian Rockies by an explorer, David Thompson. The footprints were 14 inches long and 8 inches wide. They did not resemble the prints of any known animal. There have been more than 750 alleged sightings of this creature. Bigfoot is said to look like a huge hairy ape, who walks upright on two feet, is over 8 feet tall, and weighs over 400 pounds. In 1967 a film was made of Bigfoot, but the film and other photographs have been dismissed by non-believers as those of big men dressed in ape suits.

LOCH NESS MONSTER

'Nessie' is the nickname of this creature who is said to live in Loch Ness, a lake in northern Scotland. Nessie has been described as a 30-foot long water beast with a long thin neck, a small head, and humps on its back.

The first sighting of the Loch Ness Monster was 1,500 years ago by St. Columba. Since then more than 10,000 sightings have been reported. Photographs and films have been taken of Nessie, and the Royal Air Force have verified the films stating that this creature does exist. Today, scientific instruments are being used to locate and catch the elusive Nessie who is now protected under Scottish law.

Weather

TWELVE WEATHER LEGENDS

1. Rain before seven, fine before eleven.
2. Red sky at night, shepherd's delight.
   Red sky in morning, shepherd's warning.
3. When the dew is on the grass, rain will never come to pass.
4. Heavy dews in hot weather, foretell fine weather.
5. No dew after sun, hot weather on the run.
6. A halo round the Moon tells of rain that's coming soon.
7. When the comb crackles through the hair look for weather clear and fair.
8. Thunder in Spring, cold will bring.
9. Flies will swarm before a storm.
10. If Candlemas be fair and bright,
    Winter will have another flight.
    But if Candlemas brings clouds and rain
    Winter is gone and won't come again.
11. If it rains on St. Swithin's Day (July 15) rain will persist for the next 40 days.
12. If January Kalends be summerly gay
    There'll be wintery weather till the Kalends of May.

WEATHER THERMOMETERS

The Fahrenheit thermometer scale was developed in 1714 by a German physicist named Gabriel Fahrenheit. The Fahrenheit scale fixes 32°F. as the freezing point, 212°F. as the boiling point of water.

The centigrade or Celsius scale was devised by the Swedish astronomer, Andes Celsius in 1742. Its freezing point is 0°C. Its boiling point is 100°C. The Celsius scale is used by the World Meteorological Organization.

Temperature Conversion Chart

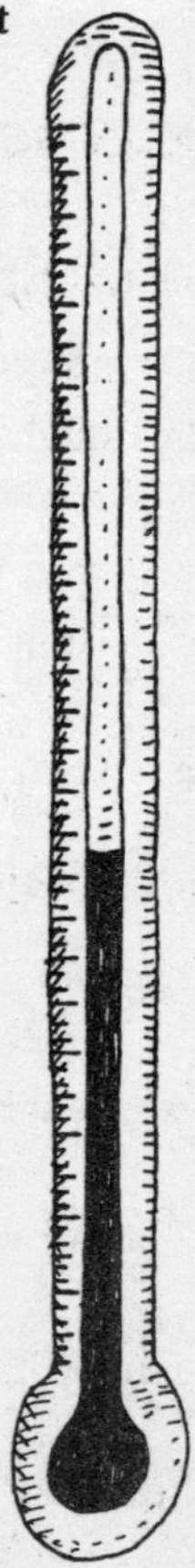

Degrees Fahrenheit	Degrees Celsius
212	100 (Water Boils)
194	90
176	80
158	70
140	60
134	56.7
122	50
104	40
86	30
68	20
50	10
32	0 (Water Freezes)
14	−10
−4	−20
−22	−30
−40	−40
−58	−50
−76	−60
−79.8	−62.1
−94	−70
−112	−80
−130	−90
−148	−100

WIND CHILL

In the winter there is a lot of talk about the wind chill factor. Wind chill occurs when the air temperature and wind combine to make the air feel colder than the temperature reading. It can be very dangerous. For example, when the outside temperature is zero degrees and the wind speed is 20 miles per hour, the wind chill makes it feel that the temperature is – 40°F.

WIND CHILL FACTOR CHART

Wind Speed (mph)	*Thermometer Reading (degrees Fahrenheit)*															
	35	*30*	*25*	*20*	*15*	*10*	*5*	*0*	*–5*	*–10*	*–15*	*–20*	*–25*	*–30*	*–35*	*–40*
5	33	27	21	19	12	7	0	–5	–10	–15	–21	–26	–31	–36	–42	–47
10	22	16	10	3	–3	–9	–15	–22	–27	–34	–40	–46	–52	–58	–64	–71
15	16	9	2	–5	–11	–18	–25	–31	–38	–45	–51	–58	–65	–72	–78	–85
20	12	4	–3	–10	–17	–24	–31	–39	–46	–53	–60	–67	–74	–81	–88	–95
25	8	1	–7	–15	–22	–29	–36	–44	–51	–59	–66	–74	–81	–88	–96	–103
30	6	–2	–10	–18	–25	–33	–41	–49	–56	–64	–71	–79	–86	–93	–101	–109
35	4	–4	–12	–20	–27	–35	–43	–52	–58	–67	–74	–82	–89	–97	–105	–113
40	3	–5	–13	–21	–29	–37	–45	–53	–60	–69	–76	–84	–92	–100	–107	–115
45	2	–6	–14	–22	–30	–38	–46	–54	–62	–70	–78	–85	–93	–102	–109	–117

WORLD WEATHER EXTREMES

Coldest Spot: Plateau Station, Antarctica with an average yearly temperature of –70°F.

Coldest Inhabited Spot: Oymyakon, Siberia, –96°F. in 1964.

Hottest Spot: Dalol, Ethiopia has an average yearly temperature of 94°F.

Sunniest Spot: The Sahara Desert where the sun shines 97 percent of the time.

Rainiest Spot: Mt. Waialeale, Hawaii with an annual average rainfall of 460 inches.

Driest Spot: Atacama Desert, Chile; has less than 1½ inches of rain a year.

Windiest Spot: Mt. Washington, New Hampshire, U.S. (In 1934 a world record wind of 231 mph swirled around this mountain top.)

Coldest Recorded Temperature: –128.6°F. in Vostok, Antarctica on August 24, 1960.

Hottest Recorded Temperature: 136°F. in El Azizia, Libya on September 13, 1922.

Greatest One Day Rainfall: Cilaos, La Reunion, Indian Ocean, 72.62 inches, March 15–16, 1952.

Longest Hot Spell: 162 consecutive days of 100°F. temperatures in Marble Bar, Australia.

Environment

ENVIRONMENTAL WORD LIST

Acid rain—Rain tainted by chemical waste which burns and harms plant and animal life.

Biodegradable—Something that can be broken down into small molecules that fit into nature's cycle.

Conservation—Careful use and protection of nature.

Ecology—The study of the natural relationship of living things to their environment.

Habitat—The place where people, animals, and plants live and grow; the total environment of air, water, and soil.

Oil spill—Accidental discharge of petroleum into bodies of water which can damage water life.

Pesticides—Substances used to control pests; too much can poison the food supply and environment.

Pollutant—Anything that dirties the air, water, or ground—thereby harming living things.

Recycle—To collect and rework used items (such as empty cans) so that materials from which the items are made can be used again.

Thermal pollution—The discharge of heated water into nature's water system which can harm plants and animals.

TEN THINGS YOU CAN DO TO HELP PROTECT OUR ENVIRONMENT

- Walk or ride a bike instead of asking for a ride.
- Don't litter, put your rubbish in the bins provided.
- Save newspapers for recycling.
- Use both sides of your writing and drawing paper.
- Be sure to turn off all water taps tightly.
- When you leave a room be sure to turn off the lights.
- Don't let the water run when you brush your teeth.
- Don't throw rubbish down the toilet.
- Use reusable cups and plates instead of paper ones.
- Plant trees.

ENVIRONMENTAL SYMBOLS

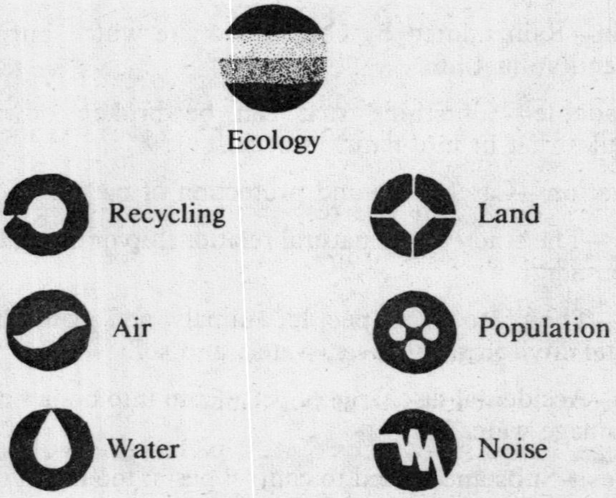

ECOLOGY ORGANIZATIONS

Friends of the Earth
377 City Road
London EC1V 1NA
(Tel: 01–837 0731)

Green Peace
36 Graham Street
London N1 8LL
(Tel: 01- 251 3022/3020)

The Woodland Trust
Autumn Park, Grantham
Lincs. NG31 6LL
(Tel: Grantham (0476) 74297)

Fauna & Flora Preservation Society
c/o Zoological Society of London
Regent's Park
London NW1 4RY
(01–722 3333)

World Wildlife Fund (UK)
Panda House
11 – 13 Ockford Road
Godalming, Surrey GU7 1QU)
(Tel: Godalming (04868) 20551)

The Wildfowl Trust
Slimbridge, Glos.
(Tel: 045 389333)

Royal Society for the Protection of Birds
The Lodge, Sandy
Beds.
(Tel: 0767 80551)

Royal Society for Nature Conservation
The Green, Nettleham
Lincs. LN2 2NR
(Tel: 0522 752326)

THE COUNTRY CODE

Farmers often allow us to walk on their land, but if we want to ensure that others can enjoy it in the future we should take care to follow the rules of courtesy and good manners. The following code is issued by the Countryside Commission:

a. Enjoy the countryside and respect its life and work.

b. Guard against all risks of fire.

c. Fasten all gates.

d. Keep your dog under close control.

e. Keep to public paths across farmland.

f. Use gates and stiles to cross fences, hedges and walls.

g. Leave livestock, crops and machinery alone.

h. Take your litter home.

i. Help to keep all water clean.

j. Protect wildlife, plants and trees.

k. Take special care on country roads.

l. Make no unnecessary noise.

A GLOSSARY OF ZOOLOGICAL TERMS

Amphibious	Able to live on both land and water.
Anthropoid Apes	The group of animals most closely related to man; gibbons, orang-utan, chimpanzee, gorilla.
Aquatic	Living in water.
Arboreal	Living in or among trees.
Carapace	The shell which covers the back of tortoises and similar animals.
Carnivorous	Flesh-eating.
Cocoon	A protective case enclosing the pupa of an insect.
Crustacean	A member of a group of animals with a hard outer shell: lobsters, prawns, crabs, etc.
Diurnal	Active during the day.
Entomology	The scientific study of insects.
Environment	The surroundings and conditions in which a plant or an animal lives.
Fauna	All the animals inhabiting a region.
Gestation	Length of time from conception to birth.
Habitat	The natural home of an animal or plant.
Herbivorous	Feeding on grasses.
Ichthyology	The scientific study of fishes.
Incubation	Keeping eggs warm until they hatch.
Indigenous	Native to the country it inhabits.
Insectivorous	Insect-eating.
Invertebrate	An animal without a backbone, such as an insect.
Iridescent	Showing changing colours as light falls on it.

Marsupial	A group of mammals born in an immature state, and developing in a pouch which contains the teats of the milk glands. Includes kangaroos, opossums, bandicoots, koalas and wombats.
Migrate	To make seasonal journeys from one part of the world to another.
Molluscs	A group of animals which have soft bodies, without a backbone, and are usually covered with a shell: snails, oysters, mussels; etc.
Nocturnal	Active during the night.
Omnivorous	Eating a diet of both animals and vegetable origin.
Predator	An animal which captures, kills and eats other animals.
Species	A single kind or sort of animal or plant.
Terrestrial	Living on the ground.
Territory	A defined area of the environment occupied and often jealously defended by an individual or group.
Ungulate	A mammal with hoofed feet.
Vertebrate	An animal possessing a backbone. The vertebrates comprise fish, amphibians, reptiles, birds and mammals.

Index